a great primitive poem — an alarum
or trumpet note ringing through the
American camp. Wonderfully the
the orientals too, considering that when
I asked him if he had read them he
answered "No." tells me about them.

I did not get far in conversation with
him — two more being present, and among
the few things which I chanced to say, I
remember that one was, in answer to him
as representing America, that I did
not think much of America or of politics
& so on — which may have been somewhat ya damper to him.

Since I have been here I find
that I am not disturbed by any brag
or egoism in his books. He may be
not the least ya braggart —
a better right to —   gods, having
                . is confident.
his a great fellow —

                    H. D. T.

LETTERS
TO A
SPIRITUAL
SEEKER

HENRY DAVID THOREAU

Edited by Bradley P. Dean

W. W. NORTON & COMPANY
New York · London

Letters 9, 36, 44, and 45: Copyright © 1966 by University of Texas Press;
reprinted from *Texas Studies in Literature and Language* with the permission
of Joseph J. Moldenhauer and University of Texas Press

Manufacturing by Quebecor World, Fairfield
Book design by Charlotte Staub
Production manager: Amanda Morrison

Library of Congress Cataloging-in-Publication Data
Thoreau, Henry David, 1817–1862.
Letters to a spiritual seeker / Henry David Thoreau ; edited by Bradley P.
Dean.—1st ed.
p. cm.
Includes bibliographical references (p.   ).
ISBN 0-393-05941-3
1. Thoreau, Henry David, 1817–1862—Correspondence. 2. Blake, Harrison G.
(Harrison Gray), 1818–1876—Correspondence. 3. Authors, American—19th
century—Correspondence. 4. Spiritual life. I. Dean, Bradley P. II. Blake,
Harrison G. (Harrison Gray), 1818–1876. III. Title.
PS3053.A3   2004
818'.309—dc22   2004010218

W. W. Norton & Company, Inc.
500 Fifth Avenue, New York, N.Y. 10110
www.wwnorton.com

W. W. Norton & Company Ltd.
Castle House, 75/76 Wells Street, London W1T 3QT

1 2 3 4 5 6 7 8 9 0

The editor dedicates his labor on this volume to

Debra Kang Dean
David Paul Kekūpaʻa Dean
Ida Mae Arrand-Dean
Frederick Paul Dean
Edith Kay Dean

Contents ☙

Introduction ⤳

HENRY DAVID THOREAU is not usually regarded as a spiritual teacher. He is best known for the literary brilliance of his masterpiece, *Walden,* and for the social and political insights of his most famous essay, "Civil Disobedience." Yet Thoreau himself clearly regarded the spiritual dimension of his writings—and, indeed, of his life—as vitally important. That dimension rarely appears in the foreground of his writings, however, and most often emerges only by implication, whereas matters of the spirit are emphatically *the* topic of consideration in the letters collected here.

No one understood the spiritual dimension of Thoreau's life and writings so clearly or so early as Harrison Gray Otis Blake, the spiritual seeker of these letters. In his first and only surviving letter to Thoreau, Blake described himself as "trembling on the brink" of a spiritual pilgrimage. Lacking the emotional and spiritual reserves for embarking on such a pilgrimage alone, he sought a teacher and recognized Thoreau as a man uniquely fitted for the task. "If I understand rightly the significance of your life," he incisively wrote to Thoreau, "this is it: You would sunder yourself from society, from the spell of institutions, customs, conventionalities, that you may lead a fresh, simple life with God. Instead of breathing a new life into the old forms, you would have a new life without and within." Blake aspired to his own "fresh, simple life with God"; Thoreau, he was convinced, could help him achieve it.

Blake's letter, written in March 1848, shows him to have been a man of considerable daring and prescience, for at this early date the man he sought out as his teacher was almost entirely unknown. Six months before receiving the letter, Thoreau had left his small house on the shore of Walden Pond; his first book, *A Week on the Concord and Merrimack Rivers*, would not be published for over a year, not until late May 1849; and *Walden*, his second book, would not be published for well over six years, in August 1854. Yet somehow Blake saw beyond the obscurity in which Thoreau existed at that time and recognized in the fledgling writer the genius he would gradually become during the course of their extraordinary thirteen-year relationship.

Late in life Blake responded to several queries from correspondents interested in learning more about his relationship with Thoreau. He confessed to one such correspondent that his initial letter to Thoreau was "[p]erhaps the best definite service I ever performed for my fellow-men" because the letter "simply recogniz[ed] Thoreau at a time when he was so little recognized. . . ." His response to another correspondent sheds important light on the Thoreau-Blake relationship and is itself an excellent brief introduction to the letters collected here:

> Our relation, as I look back on it, seems almost an impersonal one, and illustrates well his remark that "our thoughts are the epochs in our lives; all else is but as a journal of the winds that blew while we were here." His personal appearance did not interest me particularly, except as the associate of his spirit, though I felt no discord between them. When together, we had

little inclination to talk of personal matters. His aim was directed so steadily and earnestly towards what is essential in our experience, that beyond all others of whom I have known, he made but a single impression on me. Geniality, versatility, personal familiarity are, of course, agreeable in those about us, and seem necessary in human intercourse, but I did not miss them in Thoreau, who was, while living, and is still in my recollection and in what he has left to us, such an effectual witness to what is highest and most precious in life. As I re-read his letters from time to time, which I never tire of doing, I am apt to find new significance in them, am still warned and instructed by them, with more force occasionally than ever before; so that in a sense they are still in the mail, have not altogether reached me yet, and will not probably before I die. They may well be regarded as addressed to those who can read them best.

When Blake wrote to Thoreau in March 1848, he was a thirty-one-year-old widower with two young daughters, an ex-minister (Unitarian) who eked out a living by teaching private school and tutoring in Worcester, Massachusetts, twenty-six miles southwest of Thoreau's hometown of Concord. A friend wrote of him shortly after his death in 1898, "He was a perfectly typical disciple. He had the reverence for all that is good or great, the constant desire to spread its influence, and the lack of purely personal initiative, which combine to make an ideal follower."

Blake's most outstanding trait, however, was conscientiousness, which he possessed almost to a fault. At a Harvard reunion he said to a classmate, "Very glad to see you." After moving on, however, he bethought himself, returned to the fellow, and quite seriously corrected his greeting by leaving off the intensifier: "Glad to see you." On another occasion he roused his sister's household just before midnight in order to modify an inaccuracy: he had said earlier in the day that he "should go to Boston tomorrow" when he actually meant to say that he "*expected* to go to Boston tomorrow." Thoreau's townsman, the great writer and philosopher Ralph Waldo Emerson, once jokingly described Blake as the sort of man who would even return a borrowed umbrella.

Thoreau and Blake had known one another "by sight" while both attended Harvard College in Cambridge, across the Charles River from Boston. Blake graduated in 1835 but stayed on at Harvard's Divinity School until 1838, while Thoreau completed his undergraduate studies and returned to Concord in 1837.

Both young men during their Harvard years encountered the writings of various transcendentalist authors, particularly the writings of Emerson. As we shall see, Thoreau read and was profoundly influenced by Emerson's great transcendentalist manifesto, *Nature,* in the fall of 1836, at the beginning of his senior year. For his part, Blake served in the early spring of 1838 on the commencement speaker committee with two of his classmates and was very likely instrumental in that committee's decision to invite Emerson to deliver the "customary address" at their commencement on July 15. The address Emerson delivered was anything but customary, however. In fact, it was his revolutionary and now very famous "Divinity School Address." With truly marvelous audacity, Emerson admonished Blake and the other graduating divines "first of all, to go alone; to refuse the good models, even those which are sacred in the imagination of men, and dare to love God without mediator or veil."

The effect of Emerson's address on Blake appears to have been as profound as *Nature* had been on Thoreau eighteen months earlier. During the decade that followed, Blake quit the ministry, entered the teaching profession, and worshiped at Emerson's shrine, writing letters to him periodically and on occasion visiting him in Concord. During one such visit, probably in late 1844 or early 1845, Emerson introduced Blake to Thoreau, and the two men struck up a conversation.

During their conversation, the subject of astronomy came up, and Thoreau remarked that he was primarily interested in "studies relating more directly to this world." At some point Thoreau alluded to his plan to build a small house for himself in the woods somewhere nearby where he would retire "farther from our civilization," and Blake asked him "if you would feel no longings for the society of your friends." Thoreau replied, "No, I am nothing," or words to that effect, a response Blake found memorable because it indicated to him "a depth of resources, a completeness of renunciation, a poise and repose in the universe" which he found "almost inconceivable" and to which he looked up "with veneration."

Later, in the early spring of 1848, after Thoreau had returned from Walden Pond, Blake read Thoreau's brief essay on the Roman satirical poet Persius. The essay had been published eight years earlier in the transcendentalists' magazine, *The Dial*. Although fairly unremarkable to most readers, the essay contains idealistic sentiments that Blake found extremely appealing, sentiments that revived in him the "haunting impression" of Thoreau he had gotten when the two men spoke at Emerson's. "I would know of that soul which can say 'I am nothing,' " Blake told Thoreau. "I would be roused by its words to a truer and purer life." Blake's letter is a very clear appeal from a would-be disciple to a prospective master. "Speak to me in this hour as you are prompted," he enjoined Thoreau, thereby initiating the remarkable letters collected here.

➢ "What is religion?" asked Thoreau in his journal on August 18, 1858, and then emphatically scrawled his answer, "That which is never spoken."

Two days before, on August 16, the American president James Buchanan had sent the first telegraph message across the Atlantic Ocean to Britain's Queen Victoria: "Glory to God in the highest, and on earth, peace, good will to men." To celebrate this technological achievement, one of Thoreau's showier neighbors in Concord held a party the following night, August 17. Emblazoned in enormous letters across the front of his brightly illuminated house were the words "Glory to God in the highest." Thoreau was walking by when partygoers issued from the house and began exploding strings of firecrackers beneath the large display. Feeling a sense of shame, he "was inclined to pass quickly by, the ideas of indecent exposure and cant being suggested." That sentiment splashed across the façade of the house seemed to him not one "to be illuminated, but to keep dark about. A simple and genuine sentiment of reverence would not emblazon these words as on a signboard in the streets."

Religion is never spoken because the deepest truths of human experience cannot be communicated directly from person to person. Some fatal loss occurs. True prophets hit by indirection. Metaphor, parable, symbol, allegory—these and other tropes are the tools with which spiritual teachers "presume to fable of the ineffable."

In "Civil Disobedience" Thoreau wrote, "They who know of no purer sources of truth, who have traced up its stream no higher, stand, and wisely stand, by the Bible and the [U.S.] Constitution, and drink at it there with reverence and humanity; but they who behold where it comes trickling into this lake or that pool, gird up their loins once more, and continue their pilgrimage toward its fountainhead." His vision of life as a pilgrimage *toward* the fountainhead of truth is one that many will find salutary. Fundamentally, it is a spiritual vision, and every one of the world's great scriptures articulates it, each in its own fashion. The Way, the Light, the Tao, the Life. These, Thoreau believed, were all one, all Truth—each simply a different articulation of the human sense of the divine, a manifestation of the religious impulse unique to a particular time and place.

Once, while reading the scriptures of the Orient, he wrote, "I pray to be delivered from narrowness, partiality, exaggeration, bigotry. To the philosopher all sects, all nations are alike. I like Brahma, Hare Buddha, the Great Spirit, as well as God." He thought it "a sad mistake" to try to prove or even to acknowledge the personality of God. Our sense of eternal, infinite omnipotence ought not be circumscribed by mere personhood, which also implies separation and distance. Still, he understood that all human beings, himself included, are reduced to the necessity of using the trope of personality as a means of expressing and even conceiving our sense of the divine. "Every people have gods to suit their circumstances," he remarks, and then gives a specific example to illustrate his point: "[T]he Society Islanders had a god called Toahitu, 'in shape like a dog; he saved such as were in danger of falling from rocks and trees.' I think that we can do without him, as we have not much climbing to do."

Metaphorically we have a very great deal of climbing to do, indeed, as Thoreau knew. He had begun his own ascent early in his life, prompted in large part by Emerson, who lived in Concord and became Thoreau's mentor for many years. Emerson's *Nature* is a scripture of that time and place, but like all the world's great scriptures, it inspires seekers of all times and places. It inspired Thoreau.

Emerson pointed out that preceding generations had beheld God and Nature face to face, but his generation saw them only through the eyes of those earlier generations, as though God and Nature were no longer directly accessible. "Why should not we also enjoy an original relation to the universe?" he asked. "Why should not we have . . . a religion by revelation to us, and not the history of theirs?" Truth, God, Nature *are,* not were. Rather than read and base our lives upon the scriptures of previous seekers, freethinking individuals may seek the fountainhead themselves.

For the remainder of his life Thoreau strove earnestly to "enjoy an original relation to the universe." With that imperative fixed in his mind, he girded up his loins in 1836 and set out on a twenty-six-year pilgrimage that ended with his death from tuberculosis at the age of forty-four. His writings are most profitably understood as reports from along the route of his pilgrimage. For inspiration he consulted the world's great scriptures, which he read eagerly, studied carefully, and admired greatly. And, of course, he drew inspiration and information from many other sources as well: family, friends, magazines, books. Some of these varied sources he retooled for his own purposes, but he used none of them for guidance. His sole guide was his own innate sense of Truth, a sense derived from within. "Behold, the kingdom of God is within you," an old book says. Thoreau believed that.

Publicly, he never put a name to his religion, although he came very close to doing so in the "Sunday" chapter of his first book, *A Week,* where he wrote, "In my Pantheon, Pan still reigns in his pristine glory, with his ruddy face, his flowing beard, and his shaggy body, his pipe and his crook . . . for the great god Pan is not dead, as was rumored. No god ever dies. Perhaps of all the gods of New England and of ancient Greece, I am most constant at his shrine." Nature, he sensed, was imbued with divinity. "I was born to be a pantheist—if that be the name of me," he confessed to a friend in 1853.

And yet just a year later he seemed not so sure. "We soon get through with Nature," he wrote in a journal entry of May 1854. "She excites an expectation which she cannot satisfy." He had just submitted the corrected proofs of his masterpiece, *Walden,* to the publisher, and in the "Higher Laws" chapter of that book he had written, "Nature is hard to be overcome, but she must be overcome." At this point in his pilgrimage he sensed that perhaps Nature leaves off where God begins: "[T]he last of Nature is but the first of God. . . . This earth which is spread out like a map around me is but the lining of my inmost soul exposed." The true path of spiritual discovery is one of continuous exploration; a pilgrim's progress often involves retrograde movements.

One of the most redeeming aspects of Thoreau's spirituality is his steadfast insistence that spirituality is not sufficient unto itself. He was a profoundly introspective man, and he identified himself at the most fundamental level as a spirit. That is *who he was*. But he understood perfectly well that he was something more. That he was fundamentally a spirit seemed to him not at all strange or unfounded. What was strange to him was what followed from that identification given two other basic facts of his experience: first, that he as a spirit lived or dwelled within a physical body, and, second, that he as a spirit was able by virtue of that physical body to *contact* or relate to the world of matter.

This point of contact between spirit and matter was, to him, the fundamental mystery—and is also why the spiritual is not sufficient unto itself. The Christian religion, he felt, did not sufficiently consider the physical body or the world of matter. Christ, Thoreau thought, "taught mankind but imperfectly how to live; his thoughts were all directed toward another world. There is another kind of success than his. Even here we have a sort of living to get, and must buffet it somewhat longer. There are various tough problems yet to solve, and we must make shift to live, betwixt spirit and matter, such a human life as we can."

Matter mattered a great deal to Thoreau, for spiritual success would only follow in the wake of a distinctive form of material success. To most people material success implies worldly wealth, riches, a great deal of money. But to Thoreau material success was achieved by curbing the desire for an excess of the sorts of goods and riches that moth and rust might corrupt, or that thieves might steal. By simplifying our outward lives, we are freer and better able to expand and enrich our inward lives.

Another redemptive characteristic of Thoreau's spirituality is its generous and accommodating expansiveness. He detested religious creeds and doctrines as certain indicators of narrowness and bigotry. During the 1840s and early 1850s he undertook a study of the religious traditions of the East and was as impressed with them as with Western religious traditions. On the basis of his studies of the world's great religious traditions he suggested that "[i]t would be worthy of the age to print together the collected Scriptures or Sacred Writings of the several nations, the Chinese, the Hindoos, the Persians, the Hebrews, and others, as the Scripture of mankind." The "juxtaposition and comparison" of those scriptures, he thought, "might help to liberalize the faith of men." That faith of human beings he honored above any of its particular religious manifestations.

The moral earnestness of Blake's first letter to Thoreau is unmistakable, and the thirty-year-old writer responded to it by straining to be oracular. His suggestion at the close of Letter 2 that Blake send *him* some oracles in return betrays his sense of awkwardness. Blake deftly responded with questions, apparently, not oracles, and with Letter 3 Thoreau becomes more sure of himself in his new role as spiritual teacher. Not until Letter 6, however, does the master's hand begin to fit itself con-

fidently to the pen. Increasingly thereafter the ink flows effort-
lessly onto the page, often with the "infinite depth of fun" as
well as the "depth of earnestness" which a mutual friend said
characterized Thoreau's manner of conversation.

Between 1848 and 1852 Blake was unable to earn a com-
fortable living in Worcester and was forced during two of those
four years to teach in the Boston area, where there were more
students whose families could afford his modest fees. His marriage in the autumn of 1852 to one of his Worcester-area students, the daughter of a wealthy family, lifted his financial
burdens. Although free to follow his own interests, he continued to teach at his own private school for young women.

Blake and his bride purchased a house atop the hill just west
of downtown Worcester. The city at that time had a well-
deserved reputation for being politically and socially liberal, and
Blake had developed close friendships with several of the city's
intelligentsia. Preeminent among his friends was Theophilus
"Theo" Brown, a tailor by trade, a kind and gentle man by
nature, and by all accounts a superb conversationalist. Thoreau
asks at the end of Letter 5 to be remembered to Brown, who is
mentioned with increasing regularity in the letters thereafter.
Eventually, with Letter 20, Brown is brought into the dialogue
altogether, for Thoreau tells Blake, "You will allow me to consider that I correspond with [Brown] through you."

This expansion of the readership of Thoreau's letters from
Blake alone to both Blake and Brown began a discernible trend.
Blake and his circle of friends in Worcester often convened at
Brown's tailor shop on Main Street to enjoy one another's
company and discuss the issues of the day. Regulars at these

get-togethers included storekeeper Henry Harmon Chamber-
lin, hydropathic physician Seth Rogers, and three liberal minis-
ters: Thomas Wentworth Higginson, Edward Everett Hale, and
David Atwood Wasson. These seven men formed a sort of
Thoreauvian coterie in Worcester—a fan club, if you will.
When one of his longer letters arrived, Blake would send these
and perhaps other friends an invitation, one of which reads:
"Mr. H. G. O. Blake presents his compliments. The pleasure of
your company is requested at breakfast tomorrow at his home,
No. 3 Bowdoin Street, when he will read extracts from Mr.
Thoreau's latest letter."

Several of Thoreau's missives to Blake are simply "business"
letters, as Thoreau himself characterized them, but even these
are important for what they indicate about the two men's relationship. Some of these brief letters discuss the details of trips
Thoreau was making or excursions the two men planned with
one another, often with Brown or other friends. A few others
deal with lectures, for Blake seems to have exploited and even
created opportunities to have his mentor lecture in Worcester.
In fact, Thoreau delivered more lectures in Worcester, nine of
them, than in any other location outside his hometown, where
he delivered twenty-six. Blake arranged these lectures, advertised them, and on a few occasions even hosted them in his
"parlors," probably the front room of his home, which likely
opened out into an adjoining room. And, of course, Blake also
provided lodging in his home whenever Thoreau came to visit,
whether to lecture or otherwise, a favor Thoreau reciprocated
whenever Blake visited Thoreau in Concord.

Blake was mindful of the extraordinary character of

Thoreau's letters and told a friend "as early as 1859 that he was considering editing them for publication with notes and comments." Unfortunately, he never did. Unfortunately, too, he regarded his own letters to Thoreau as important only because they prompted Thoreau's responses. Blake had inherited his letters to Thoreau in 1876, when Thoreau's younger sister bequeathed to him her brother's manuscripts. Late in life Blake lent all of his own letters to the early Thoreau biographer Franklin Benjamin Sanborn, at whose death the letters were very likely destroyed. The only one that survived—and that heavily excised—was the initial one, which appears in this collection as Letter 1. All forty-nine of the remaining letters collected here are Thoreau's, and they are all addressed to Blake.

Or are they?

As we have seen, during the thirteen-year period in which these letters were written, they gradually evolved from private communications between two men to semipublic documents shared within a small community of friends. Thoreau surely knew about the gatherings of the faithful at Blake's invitation following the delivery of each of his longer letters. So he wrote many of his later letters with the knowledge that his audience had grown beyond Blake and Brown to that coterie of friends in Worcester. And given his character, Blake very likely informed Thoreau about his idea of publishing the letters.

Thoreau began this trend in December 1854 by expanding his audience to include Brown. The trajectory of the trend is unmistakable and, perhaps, inevitable—and the recipient of these letters knew it. In a very real sense, these letters are *not* addressed to H. G. O. Blake of No. 3 Bowdoin Street, Worcester, Massachusetts. They are addressed, as Blake himself stated, "to those who can read them best."

These letters have waited more than one hundred and forty years to appear together in their own separate volume. They provided inspiration and encouragement to one spiritual seeker those many years ago, and through that man they inspired and encouraged a small group of equally high-minded friends. If not inevitable, surely it is fitting that these letters are now available to a still-wider audience, to new generations of seekers who can enjoy and benefit from the masterful insights of a great spiritual teacher.

BRADLEY P. DEAN
West Peterborough, New Hampshire

A Note on the Texts ⤜

THE TEXTS OF LETTERS 1–8, 10–11, 12–35, 37–43, and 46–50 are reprinted from *The Correspondence of Henry David Thoreau*, edited by Walter Harding and Carl Bode (New York: New York University Press, 1958). The texts of Letters 9, 36, 44, and 45 are reprinted with the permission of the University of Texas Press from Joseph J. Moldenhauer, "Thoreau to Blake: Four Letters Re-edited," *Texas Studies in Literature and Language* 8 (Spring 1966): 43–62. The texts of the two enclosures to Letter 11 are reprinted from Henry D. Thoreau, *Letters to Various Persons*, edited by Ralph Waldo Emerson (Boston: Ticknor and Fields, 1865), although I have incorporated into nine of the paragraphs of "Love" ("The maiden conceals . . . light as a flame") the textual differences noted in Joseph J. Moldenhauer, "Textual Supplement to Thoreau's Essay on 'Love,'" *Thoreau Society Bulletin* 149 (Fall 1979): 6–7.

I have applied a fairly conservative editorial policy because preserving such "irregularities" as ampersands and Thoreau's liberal use of dashes preserves a more complete sense of his epistolary style and the immediacy of his composition process. To enhance the reading experience, however, I have silently regularized certain anomalies from my sources, such as removing the square brackets from words which Blake cut from the manuscript letters in order to give Thoreau's autograph to collectors (inscribing the missing words in his own hand elsewhere on the manuscript leaf), removing editorially supplied supplemental information such as first names and completing abbreviations, adding some missing punctuation, and supplying a space after a few terminal dashes. I have also silently corrected Thoreau's misspellings, although I retain spellings represented in one or another of the lexicons he is known to have used. All square brackets in the text of the letters are my own and enclose editorially supplied information. I maintain a detailed list of the differences between the sources listed above and the texts as presented in this volume at www.bradleypdean.com/seeker.

HARRISON G. O. BLAKE
Courtesy, American Antiquarian Society

HENRY DAVID THOREAU
Courtesy, Thoreau Society

*Letters
to a
Spiritual Seeker*

✺ Letter One

[From Harrison G. O. Blake; March 1848; Worcester, Massachusetts]

In March 1848 Henry David Thoreau (1817–1862) was thirty years of age, Harrison Gray Otis Blake (1816–1898) a year older. After residing at Walden twenty-six months, Thoreau had left his retreat at the pond on September 6, 1847, six months before receiving this letter. While there he had written most of the manuscript for his first book, *A Week on the Concord and Merrimack Rivers,* which would not see publication until May 1849, and had written a complete draft of his second and most famous book, *Walden,* which remained unpublished until August 1854. Those were the only two books he published during his lifetime. As he mentions in Letter 3, he was at this time living in the Emerson household, where he kept Lidian Emerson (1802–1892) company and served as handyman while her husband Ralph Waldo Emerson (1803–1882) lectured in England. Forty-two years after writing this letter Blake remarked, "Perhaps the best definite service I ever performed for my fellow-men was, like our best services generally, the unintended one of simply recognizing Thoreau at a time when he was yet so little recognized, giving him, as he said, 'an opportunity to live,' making by my letters an occasion for his. . . ." I have added the paragraph breaks to this letter.

✺ It [Thoreau's essay "Aulus Persius Flaccus"] has revived in me a haunting impression of you, which I carried away from some spoken words of yours. . . .

When I was last in Concord, you spoke of retiring farther from our civilization. I asked you if you would feel no longings for the society of your friends. Your reply was in substance, "No, I am nothing."

That reply was memorable to me. It indicated a depth of resources, a completeness of renunciation, a poise and repose in the universe, which to me is almost inconceivable; which in you seemed domesticated, and to which I look up with veneration. I would know of that soul which can say "I am nothing." I would be roused by its words to a truer and purer life.

Upon me seems to be dawning with new significance the idea that God is here; that we have but to bow before Him in profound submission at every moment, and He will fill our souls with his presence. In this opening of the soul to God, all duties seem to centre; what else have we to do? . . .

If I understand rightly the significance of your life, this is it: You would sunder yourself from society, from the spell of institutions, customs, conventionalities, that you may lead a fresh, simple life with God. Instead of breathing a new life into the old forms, you would have a new life without and within. There is something sublime to me in this attitude,—far as I may be from it myself. . . .

Speak to me in this hour as you are prompted. . . .

I honor you because you abstain from action, and open your soul that you may *be* somewhat. Amid a world of noisy, shallow actors it is noble to stand aside and say, "I will simply *be*." Could I plant myself at once upon the truth, reducing my wants to their minimum, . . . I should at once be brought nearer to nature, nearer to my fellow-men,—and life would be infinitely richer. But, alas! I shiver on the brink. . . .

ᔧ Letter Two

March 27, 1848, Monday; Concord, Massachusetts

Concord, March 27, 1848.

I am glad to hear that any words of mine, though spoken so long ago that I can hardly claim identity with their author, have reached you. It gives me pleasure, because I have therefore reason to suppose that I have uttered what concerns men, and that it is not in vain that man speaks to man. This is the value of literature. Yet those days are so distant, in every sense, that I have had to look at that page again, to learn what was the tenor of my thoughts then. I should value that article, however, if only because it was the occasion of your letter.

I do believe that the outward and the inward life correspond; that if any should succeed to live a higher life, others would not know of it; that difference and distance are one. To set about living a true life is to go [on] a journey to a distant country, gradually to find ourselves surrounded by new scenes and men; and as long as the old are around me, I know that I am not in any true sense living a new or a better life. The outward is only the outside of that which is within. Men are not concealed under habits, but are revealed by them; they are their true clothes. I care not how curious a reason they may give for their abiding by them. Circumstances are not rigid and unyielding, but our habits are rigid. We are apt to speak vaguely sometimes, as if a divine life were to be grafted on to or built over this present as a suitable foundation. This might do if we could so build over our old life as to exclude from it all the warmth of our affection, and addle it, as the thrush builds over the cuckoo's egg, and lays her own atop, and hatches that only; but the fact is, we—so there is the partition—hatch them both, and the cuckoo's always by a day first, and that young bird crowds the young thrushes out of the nest. No. Destroy the cuckoo's egg, or build a new nest.

Change is change. No new life occupies the old bodies;—they decay. *It* is born, and grows, and flourishes. Men very pathetically inform the old, accept and wear it. Why put it up with the almshouse when you may go to heaven? It is embalming,—no. more. Let alone your ointments and your linen swathes, and go into an infant's body. You see in the catacombs of Egypt the result of that experiment,—that is the end of it.

I do believe in simplicity. It is astonishing as well as sad, how many trivial affairs even the wisest man thinks he must attend to in a day; how singular an affair he thinks he must omit. When the mathematician would solve a difficult problem, he first frees the equation of all encumbrances, and reduces it to its simplest terms. So simplify the problem of life, distinguish the necessary and the real. Probe the earth to see where your main roots run. I would stand upon facts. Why not see,—use our eyes? Do men know nothing? I know many men who, in common things, are not to be deceived; who trust no moonshine; who count their money correctly, and know how to invest it; who are said to be prudent and knowing, who yet will stand at a desk the greater part of their lives, as cashiers in banks, and glimmer and rust and finally go out there. If they *know* anything, what under the sun do they do that for? Do they know what *bread* is? or what it is for? Do they know what life is? If they *knew* something, the places which know them now would know them no more forever.

This, our respectable daily life, in which the man of common sense, the Englishman of the world,[1] stands so squarely, and on which our institutions are founded, is in fact the veriest illusion, and will vanish like the baseless fabric of a vision;[2] but that faint glimmer of reality which sometimes illuminates the darkness of daylight for all men, reveals something more solid and enduring than adamant, which is in fact the corner-stone of the world.

Men cannot conceive of a state of things so fair that it cannot be realized. Can any man honestly consult his experience and say that it is so? Have we any facts to appeal to when we say that our dreams are premature? Did you ever hear of a man who had striven all his life faithfully and singly toward an object and in no measure obtained it? If a man constantly aspires, is he not elevated? Did ever a man try heroism, magnanimity, truth, sincerity, and find that there was no advantage in them? that it was a vain endeavor? Of course we do not expect that our paradise will be a garden. We know not what we ask.[3] To look at literature;—how many fine thoughts has every man had! how few fine thoughts are expressed! Yet we never have a fantasy so subtle and ethereal, but that *talent merely*, with more resolution and faithful persistency, after a thousand failures, might fix and engrave it in distinct and enduring words, and we should see that our dreams are the solidest facts that we know. But I speak not of dreams.

What can be expressed in words can be expressed in life.

My actual life is a fact in view of which I have no occasion to congratulate myself, but for my faith and aspiration I have respect. It is from these that I speak. Every man's position is in fact too simple to be described. I have sworn no oath. I have no designs on society—or nature—or God. I am simply what I am, or I begin to be that. I *live* in the *present*. I only remember the past—and anticipate the future. I love to live, I love reform better than its modes. There is no history of how bad became better. I believe something, and there is nothing else but that. I know that I am—I know that another is who knows more than I who takes interest in me, whose creature and yet whose kindred, in one sense, am I. I know that the enterprise is worthy— I know that things work well. I have heard no bad news.

As for positions—as for combinations and details—what are they? In clear weather when we look into the heavens, what do we see, but the sky and the sun?

If you would convince a man that he does wrong do right. But do not care to convince him.— Men will believe what they see. Let them see.[4]

Pursue, keep up with, circle round and round your life as a dog does his master's chaise. Do what you love. Know your own bone; gnaw at it, bury it, unearth it, and gnaw it still. Do not be too moral. You may cheat yourself out of much life so. Aim above morality. Be not *simply* good—be good for something.—All fables indeed have their morals, but the innocent enjoy the story.

Let nothing come between you and the light. Respect men as brothers only. When you travel to the celestial city, carry no letter of introduction. When you knock ask to see God— none of the servants. In what concerns you much do not think that you have companions—know that you are alone in the world.

Thus I write at random. I need to see you, and I trust I shall, to correct my mistakes. Perhaps you have some oracles for me.

Henry Thoreau.

ᵗᵛ *Letter Three*

May 2, 1848, Tuesday; Concord, Massachusetts

The quotation beginning this letter—"We must have our bread"—is the first clear indication that Thoreau often and perhaps usually wrote on topics of Blake's choosing. In other words, his letters should be understood as one side of what was actually a dialogue between the two men.

Concord, May 2, 1848.

"We must have our bread." But what is our bread? Is it baker's bread? Methinks it should be very *home-made* bread. What is our meat? Is it butcher's meat? What is that which we *must* have? Is that bread which we are now earning sweet? Is it not bread which has been suffered to sour, and then been sweetened with an alkali, which has undergone the vinous, acetous, and sometimes the putrid fermentation, and then been whitened with vitriol? Is this the bread which we must have? Man must earn his bread by the sweat of his brow,[1] truly, but also by the sweat of his brain within his brow. The body can feed the body only. I have tasted but little bread in my life. It has been mere grub and provender for the most part. Of bread that nourished the brain and the heart, scarcely any. There is absolutely none even on the tables of the rich.

There is not one kind of food for all men. You must and you will feed those faculties which you exercise. The laborer whose body is weary does not require the same food with the scholar whose brain is weary. Men should not labor foolishly like brutes, but the brain and the body should always, or as much as possible, work and rest together, and then the work will be of such a kind that when the body is hungry the brain will be hungry also, and the same food will suffice for both; otherwise the food which repairs the waste energy of the overwrought body will oppress the sedentary brain, and the degenerate scholar will come to esteem all food vulgar, and all getting a living drudgery.

How shall we earn our bread is a grave question; yet it is a sweet and inviting question. Let us not shirk it, as is usually done. It is the most important and practical question which is put to man. Let us not answer it hastily. Let us not be content to get our bread in some gross, careless, and hasty manner. Some men go a-hunting, some a-fishing, some a-gaming, some to war; but none have so pleasant a time as they who in earnest seek to earn their bread. It is true actually as it is true really; it is true materially as it is true spiritually, that they who seek honestly and sincerely, with all their hearts and lives and strength, to earn their bread, do earn it, and it is sure to be very sweet to them. A very little bread,—a very few crumbs are enough, if it be of the right quality, for it is infinitely nutritious. Let each man, then, earn at least a crumb of bread for his body before he dies, and know the taste of it,—that it is identical with the bread of life,[2] and that they both go down at one swallow.

Our bread need not ever be sour or hard to digest. What Nature is to the mind she is also to the body. As she feeds my imagination, she will feed my body; for what she says she means, and is ready to do. She is not simply beautiful to the poet's eye. Not only the rainbow and sunset are beautiful, but to be fed and clothed, sheltered and warmed aright, are equally beautiful and inspiring. There is not necessarily any gross and ugly fact which may not be eradicated from the life of man. We should endeavor practically in our lives to correct all the defects which our imagination detects.[3] The heavens are as deep as our aspirations are high. So high as a tree aspires to grow, so high it will find an atmosphere suited to it. Every man should stand for a force which is perfectly irresistible. How can any man be weak who dares *to be* at all? Even the tenderest plants force their way up through the hardest earth, and the crevices of rocks; but a man no material power can resist. What a wedge, what a beetle,[4] what a catapult, is an *earnest* man! What can resist him?

It is a momentous fact that a man may be good, or he may be *bad*; his life may be *true*, or it may be *false*; it may be either a shame or a glory to him. The good man builds himself up; the bad man destroys himself.

But whatever we do we must do confidently (if we are timid, let us, then, act timidly), not expecting more light, but having light enough. If we confidently expect more, then let us wait for it. But what is this which we have? Have we not already waited? Is this the beginning of time? Is there a man who does not see clearly beyond, though only a hair's breadth beyond where he at any time stands?

If one hesitates in his path, let him not proceed. Let him respect his doubts, for doubts, too, may have some divinity in them. That we have but little faith is not sad, but that we have but little faithfulness.[5] By faithfulness faith is earned. When, in the progress of a life, a man swerves, though only by an angle infinitely small, from his proper and allotted path (and this is never done quite unconsciously even at first; in fact, that was his broad and scarlet sin,[6]—ah, he knew of it more than he can tell), then the drama of his life turns to tragedy, and makes haste to its fifth act.[7] When once we thus fall behind ourselves, there is no accounting for the obstacles which rise up in our path, and no one is so wise as to advise, and no one so powerful as to aid us while we abide on that ground. Such are cursed with *duties, and the neglect of their duties.* For such the decalogue[8] was made, and other far more voluminous and terrible codes.

These departures,—who have not made them?—for they are as faint as the parallax of a fixed star,[9] and at the commencement we say they are nothing,—that is, they originate in a kind of sleep and forgetfulness of the soul when it is naught. A man cannot be too circumspect in order to keep in the straight road, and be sure that he sees all that he may at any time see, that so he may distinguish his true path.

You ask if there is no doctrine of sorrow in my philosophy. Of acute sorrow I suppose that I know comparatively little. My saddest and most genuine sorrows are apt to be but transient regrets. The place of sorrow is supplied, perchance, by a certain hard and proportionately barren indifference. I am of kin to the sod, and partake largely of its dull patience,—in winter expecting the sun of spring. In my cheapest moments I am apt to think that it is not my business to be "seeking the spirit,"[10] but as much its business to be seeking me. I know very well what Goethe meant when he said that he never had a chagrin but he made a poem out of it.[11] I have altogether too much patience of this kind. I am too easily contented with a slight and almost animal happiness. My happiness is a good deal like that of the woodchucks.

Methinks I am never quite committed, never wholly the creature of my moods, being always to some extent their critic.[12] My only integral experience is in my vision. I see, perchance, with more integrity than I feel.

But I need not tell you what manner of man I am,—my virtues or my vices. You can guess if it is worth the while; and I do not discriminate them well.

I do not write this time at my hut in the woods. I am at present living with Mrs. Emerson, whose house is an old home of mine, for company during Mr. Emerson's absence.

You will perceive that I am as often talking to myself, perhaps, as speaking to you.

❧ Letter Four

April 17, 1849, Tuesday; Concord, Massachusetts

During the preceding five months Thoreau had on six occasions delivered one or another of his three *Walden* lectures in Portland, Maine, and in the Massachusetts towns of Concord, Lincoln, Salem, and Gloucester. Blake had probably arranged for him to deliver all three *Walden* lectures in Worcester on three successive Friday evenings at 7:30 p.m., the first in City Hall on April 20, the other two in Brinley Hall on April 27 and May 3. The previous month Thoreau contracted with James Munroe and Company of Boston to publish *A Week* at his own expense, with *Walden* to be published shortly afterward. He had also agreed to write up his February 1848 lecture on "Resistance to Civil Government" (later retitled "Civil Disobedience") for publication in May. So during this time he was extremely busy preparing his manuscripts and correcting proofs. His older sister Helen was also struggling through a final bout with tuberculosis at this time. She succumbed to the disease on June 14. Thoreau rode the Fitchburg Railroad fifteen miles northwest to Groton, Massachusetts, where he changed to the Worcester & Nashua Railroad. The mention of Emerson is explained by the fact that Emerson traveled extensively as a professional lecturer and was therefore very familiar with railroad schedules and routes.

Concord Ap. 17th 1849

Dear Sir,

It is my intention to leave Concord for Worcester, via Groton, at 12 o'clock on Friday of this week. Mr Emerson tells me that it will take about two hours to go by this way. At any rate I shall try to secure 3 or 4 hours in which to see you & Worcester before the lecture.

Yrs in haste

Henry D. Thoreau

🎋 *Letter Five*

After sending off his corrected proofs of *A Week*, which had been published at the end of May, Thoreau had returned with redoubled energy to his manuscript of *Walden*, whose publication had been announced on a page at the end of *A Week*. But the commercial failure of *A Week*, perhaps not yet apparent in early August, was to delay *Walden*'s appearance until August 1854.

Concord, August 10, 1849

Mr. Blake,—

I write now chiefly to say, before it is too late, that I shall be glad to see you in Concord, and will give you a chamber, etc., in my father's house,[1] and as much of my poor company as you can bear.

I am in too great haste this time to speak to your, or out of my, condition. I might say,—you might say,—comparatively speaking, be not anxious to avoid poverty.[2] In this way the wealth of the universe may be securely invested. What a pity if we do not live this short time according to the laws of the long time,—the eternal laws! Let us see that we stand erect here, and do not lie along by our *whole length* in the dirt. Let our meanness be our footstool, not our cushion. In the midst of this labyrinth let us live a *thread*[3] of life. We must act with so rapid and resistless a purpose in *one* direction, that our vices will necessarily trail behind. The nucleus of a comet is almost a star. Was there ever a genuine dilemma? The laws of earth are for the feet, or inferior man; the laws of heaven are for the head, or superior man; the latter are the former sublimed and expanded, even as radii from the earth's centre go on diverging into space. Happy the man who observes the heavenly and the terrestrial law in just proportion; whose every faculty, from the soles of his feet to the crown of his head, obeys the law of its level; who neither stoops nor goes on tiptoe, but lives a balanced life, acceptable to nature and to God.

These things I say; other things I do.

I am sorry to hear that you did not receive my book[4] earlier. I addressed it and left it in Munroe's shop to be sent to you immediately, on the twenty-sixth of May, before a copy had been sold.

Will you remember me to Mr. Brown,[5] when you see him next: he is well remembered by

Henry Thoreau.

I still owe you a worthy answer.

🪶 Letter Six

November 20, 1849, Tuesday; Concord, Massachusetts

This fall and winter was an incredibly busy and important time for Thoreau. As he mentions in this letter, he had established a productive routine of reading and writing during mornings and evenings with a long walk in the afternoon. But that routine must have been regularly disrupted as a consequence of the commercial failure of *A Week*, which by November was a settled fact and which left Thoreau with a debt of almost three hundred dollars—about a year's wages for the average working male at the time. To begin paying off his debt (it was not fully paid until late 1853) he worked long hours in his family's pencil factory and peddled finished pencils as well. Although he seriously considered speculating in cranberries, he dropped that scheme when he found that it would not pay. Instead, he announced his services as a professional surveyor. He had purchased surveying equipment years before, when teaching with his older brother John (1814–1842), in order to give his students a practical application of mathematics, and he had used the equipment while at Walden to produce a highly detailed survey of the pond. He had even done a small surveying job for Emerson in May 1849. But now he purchased a surveyor's handbook and took on two large surveying jobs, one of which lasted throughout the winter. The previous month he and William Ellery Channing (1817–1901) had gone on a five-day excursion to Cape Cod, and he immediately began drafting a lecture based on the trip, completing a draft by December. In September he had requested and received borrowing privileges at the Harvard College Library. He used those privileges to begin researching early New England history, in part to supplement his Cape Cod lectures. In 1843 he had conducted research on graphite, the principal ingredient used to make pencils, and had dramatically improved the graphite-grinding machinery in the family's mill. As a result of his ingenuity, the family business by 1849 had effected a transition from the manufacture of pencils to supplying powdered graphite to electrotypers, a transition which resulted in sufficient prosperity for the family to purchase a commodious house on Main Street in Concord. Although they purchased the house in November 1849, repairs and improvements delayed the move for a year. Finally, during this difficult period Thoreau's relationship with Emerson degenerated badly. Emerson had encouraged Thoreau to publish *A Week* at his own expense but had criticized the book after it was published. Naturally, Thoreau felt betrayed by his erstwhile mentor, and although they continued to be on fairly good terms, their friendship never fully recovered.

Concord Nov. 20th 1849

Mr Blake,

I have not forgotten that I am your debtor. When I read over your letters, as I have just done, I feel that I am unworthy to have received or to answer them, though they are addressed, as I would have them to the ideal of me. It behooves me, if I would reply, to speak out of the rarest part of myself.

At present I am subsisting on certain wild flowers which Nature wafts to me, which unaccountably sustain me, and make my apparently poor life rich. Within a year my walks have extended themselves, and almost every afternoon (I read, or write, or make pencils, in the forenoon, and by the last means get a living for my body) I visit some new hill or pond or wood many miles distant. I am astonished at the wonderful retirement through which I move, rarely meeting a man in these excursions, never seeing one similarly engaged, unless it be my companion,[1] when I have one. I cannot help feeling that of all the human inhabitants of nature hereabouts, only we two have leisure to admire and enjoy our inheritance.

"Free in this world, as the birds in the air, disengaged from every kind of chains, those who have practiced the *yoga* gather in Brahma the certain fruit of their works."[2]

Depend upon it that rude and careless as I am, I would fain practise the *yoga* faithfully.

"The yogin, absorbed in contemplation, contributes in his degree to creation: he breathes a divine perfume, he hears wonderful things. Divine forms traverse him without tearing him, and united to the nature which is proper to him, he goes, he acts, as animating original matter."[3]

To some extent, and at rare intervals, even I am a yogin.

I know little about the affairs of Turkey,[4] but I am sure that I know something about barberries and chest nuts of which I have collected a store this fall. When I go to see my neighbor he will formally communicate to me the latest news from Turkey, which he read in yesterday's Mail—how Turkey by this time looks determined, & Lord Palmerston— Why, I would rather talk of the bran, which, unfortunately, was sifted out of my bread this morning and thrown away. It is a fact which lies nearer to me. The newspaper gossip with which our hosts abuse our ears is as far from a true hospitality as the viands which they set before us. We did not need them to feed our bodies; and the news can be bought for a penny.[5] We want the inevitable news, be it sad or cheering—wherefore and by what means they are extant, this *new* day. If they are well let them whistle and dance; if they are dyspeptic, it is their duty to complain, that so they may in any case be *entertaining*. If words are invented to conceal thought,[6] I think that newspapers are a great improvement on a bad invention. Do not suffer your life to be taken by newspapers.

I thank you for your hearty appreciation of my book. I am glad to have had such a long talk with you, and that you had patience to listen to me to the end. I think that I have the advantage of you, for I chose my own mood, and in one sense your mood too, that is a quiet and attentive reading mood. Such advantage has the writer over the talker. I am sorry that you did not come to Concord in your vacation. Is it not time for another vacation? I am here yet, and Concord is here.

You will have found out by this time who it is that writes this, and will be glad to have you write, to him, without his subscribing himself,

Henry D. Thoreau

P.S. It is so long since I have seen you, that as you will perceive, I have to speak as it were *in vacuum,* as if I were sounding hollowly for an echo, & it did not make much odds what kind of a sound I made. But the gods do not hear my rude or discordant sound, as we learn from the echo; and I know that the nature toward which I launch these sounds is so rich that it will modulate anew and wonderfully improve my rudest strain.

ᨠ Letter Seven

April 3, 1850, Wednesday; Concord, Massachusetts

Thoreau's studies in early New England history broadened into a serious interest in early Native American history that was to last the remainder of his life. He had begun recording notes from his reading on these topics in two notebooks, his "Indian Book" notes quickly spilling into several successive notebooks. During this same period he also began maintaining a "Commonplace Book" to record extracts from his reading in natural history, another lifelong interest. With the failure of *A Week*, he had laid his *Walden* manuscript aside, going back to it only occasionally to revise it slightly. His surveying business proved lucrative enough to enable him to purchase additional equipment this spring, and during the winter he had delivered his "Excursion to Cape Cod" lecture on four occasions, receiving pay for only two of those. Blake, in an effort to increase his own income, had by this time moved from Worcester, where there were not enough students to enable him to make a decent living, to Milton, Massachusetts, six miles south of downtown Boston. He taught in Milton with Christopher A. Greene (1816–1853), who had edited the short-lived reform journal *Plain Speaker*, was a friend of Thoreau's friend and townsman the educator Amos Bronson Alcott (1799–1888), and had partnered in 1841 with William M. Chace or Chase (1814–1862) in a utopian farm community.

Concord, April 3, 1850.

Mr. Blake,—

I thank you for your letter, and I will endeavor to record some of the thoughts which it suggests, whether pertinent or not. You speak of poverty and dependence. Who are poor and dependent? Who are rich and independent? When was it that men agreed to respect the appearance and not the reality? Why should the appearance *appear*? Are we well acquainted, then, with the reality?

There is none who does not lie hourly in the respect he pays to false appearance. How sweet it would be to treat men and things, for an hour, for just what they are! We wonder that the sinner does not confess his sin. When we are weary with travel, we lay down our load and rest by the wayside. So, when we are weary with the burden of life, why do we not lay down this load of falsehoods which we have volunteered to sustain, and be refreshed as never mortal was? Let the beautiful laws prevail. Let us not weary ourselves by resisting them. When we would rest our bodies we cease to support them; we recline on the lap of earth. So, when we would rest our spirits, we must recline on the Great Spirit.[1] Let things alone; let them weigh what they will; let them soar or fall. To succeed in letting only one thing alone in a winter morning, if it be only one poor frozen-thawed apple[2] that hangs on a tree, what a glorious achievement! Methinks it lightens through the dusky universe. What an infinite wealth we have discovered! God reigns, *i.e.*, when we take a liberal view,— when a liberal view is presented us.

Let God alone if need be. Methinks, if I loved him more, I should keep him,—I should keep myself rather,—at a more respectful distance. It is not when I am going to meet him, but when I am just turning away and leaving him alone, that I discover that God is. I say, God. I am not sure that that is the name. You will know whom I mean.

If for a moment we make way with our petty selves, wish no ill to anything, apprehend no ill, cease to be but as the crystal which reflects a ray,—what shall we not reflect! What a universe will appear crystallized and radiant around us!

I should say, let the Muse lead the Muse,—let the understanding lead the understanding,[3] though in any case it is the farthest forward which leads them both. If the Muse accompany, she is no muse, but an amusement. The Muse should lead like a star which is very far off; but that does not imply that we are to follow foolishly, falling into sloughs[4] and over precipices, for it is not foolishness, but understanding, which is to follow, which the Muse is appointed to lead, as a fit guide of a fit follower.

Will you live? or will you be embalmed? Will you live, though it be astride of a sunbeam;[5] or will you repose safely in the catacombs[6] for a thousand years? In the former case, the worst accident that can happen is that you may break your neck. Will you break your heart, your soul, to save your neck? Necks and pipe-stems are fated to be broken. Men make a great ado about the folly of demanding too much of life (or of eternity?), and of endeavoring to live according to that demand. It is much ado about nothing.[7] No harm ever came from that quarter. I am not afraid that I shall exaggerate the value and significance of life, but that I shall not be up to the occasion which it is. I shall be sorry to remember that I was there, but noticed nothing remarkable,—not so much as a prince in disguise;[8] lived in the golden age[9] a hired man; visited Olympus[10] even, but fell asleep after dinner, and did not hear the conversation of the gods. I lived in Judæa eighteen hundred years ago,[11] but I never knew that there was such a one as Christ among my contemporaries! If there is anything more glorious than a congress of men a-framing or amending of a constitution going on, which I suspect there is, I desire to see the morning papers. I am greedy of the faintest rumor, though it were got by listening at the key-hole. I will dissipate myself in that direction.

I am glad to know that you find what I have said on Friendship[12] worthy of attention. I wish I could have the benefit of your criticism; it would be a rare help to me.[13] Will you not communicate it?

❧ *Letter Eight*

May 28, 1850, Tuesday; Concord, Massachusetts

Concord May 28 1850

Mr Blake,

I "never found any contentment in the life which the newspapers record"—any thing of more value than the cent which
they cost. Contentment in being covered with dust an inch
deep! We who walk the streets and hold time together, are but
the refuse of ourselves, and that life is for the shells of us—
of our body & our mind—for our scurf—a thoroughly *scurvy*[1]
life. It is coffee made of coffee-grounds the twentieth time,
which was only coffee the first time—while the living water
leaps and sparkles by our doors. I know some who in their
charity give their coffee-grounds to the poor! We demanding
news, and putting up with *such* news! Is it a new convenience
or a new accident or rather a new perception of the truth that
we want?

You say that "the serene hours in which Friendship, Books,
Nature, Thought, seem above primary considerations, visit you
but faintly"— Is not the attitude of expectation[2] somewhat
divine?—a sort of home-made divineness? Does it not compel
a kind of sphere music[3] to attend on it? And do not its satis-
factions merge at length by insensible degrees in the enjoyment
of the thing expected?

What if I should forget to write about my not writing. It is
not worth the while to make that a theme. It is as if I had written every day— It is as if I had never written before—I won-

der that you think so much about it, for not writing is the most like writing in my case of anything I know.

Why will you not relate to me your dream? That would be to realize it somewhat. You tell me that you dream, but not what you dream.— I can *guess* what comes to pass. So do the frogs dream.[4] Would that I knew what. I have never found out whether they are awake or asleep—whether it is day or night with them.

I am preaching, mind you, to bare walls, that is to myself; and if you have chanced to come in and occupy a pew—do not think that my remarks are directed at you particularly, and so slam the seat in disgust. This discourse was written long before these exciting times.

Some absorbing employment on your higher ground—your upland farm, whither no cartpath leads— but where you mount alone with your hoe[5]—where the life-ever-lasting grows—you raise a crop which needs not to be brought down into the valley to a market, which you barter for heavenly products.

Do you separate distinctly enough the support of your body from that of your essence? By how distinct a course commonly are these two ends attained! Not that they should not be attained by one & the same means—that indeed is the rarest success—but there is no half and half about it.

I shall be glad to read my lecture[6] to a small audience in Worcester, such as you describe, and will only require that my expenses be paid. If only the parlor be large enough for an echo, and the audience will embarrass themselves with hearing as much as the lecturer would otherwise embarrass himself with reading. But I warn you that this is no better calculated for a promiscuous audience than the last two which I read to you.[7] It requires in every sense a concordant audience.

I will come on Saturday next and spend Sunday with you, if you wish it. Say so if you do.

Drink deep or taste not of the Pierian spring.[8] Be not deterred by melancholy on the path which leads to immortal health & joy. When they tasted of the water of the river over which they were to go, they thought that tasted a little bitterish to the palate, but it proved sweeter when it was down.[9]

H D T

⚘ Letter Nine

August 9, 1850, Friday; Concord, Massachusetts

Probably to supplement his lectures, Thoreau had visited Cape Cod again in late June, this time alone. He described the ocean in his lectures as a "vast morgue," an association that was doubtless heightened when, at Emerson's request, he left Concord on July 23 to search for the remains and personal effects of the well-known author Margaret Fuller (1810–1850), who with her husband, Giovanni Angelo, the Marquis of Ossoli (d. 1850), and their young son, Angelo (1848–1850), had perished in a shipwreck on July 19 off the coast of Fire Island, a barrier island off Long Island. The bodies of Fuller and Ossoli were never recovered. By the time Thoreau arrived, Angelo had already been buried and the ship's wreckage had been plundered, so his search was largely fruitless. He returned to Concord on July 29. Late in August the Thoreau family moved to the newly remodeled house on Main Street, where Thoreau occupied the third-floor attic. He continued, for the most part, to ignore his *Walden* manuscript. Although one scholar believes that Blake moved from Milton back to Worcester between July 22 and August 11, the fact that Blake's colleague in Milton, Christopher Greene, hand-carried this letter to Blake suggests that the move did not take place until a somewhat later date.

H. G. O. Blake
Care of Mr. *C. A. Greene*
Milton Mass.

Concord Aug. 9th 1850

Mr Blake,

I received your letter just as I was rushing to Fire Island Beach to recover what remained of Margaret Fuller and read it on the way. That event and its train, as much as anything, have prevented my answering it before. It is wisest to speak when you are spoken to. I will now endeavor to reply at the risk of having nothing to say.

I find that actual events, notwithstanding the singular prominence which we all allow them, are far less real than the creations of my imagination. They are truly visionary and insignificant—all that we commonly call life & death—and affect me less than my dreams. This petty stream which from time to time swells & carries away the mills and bridges of our habitual life—and that mightier stream or ocean on which we securely float—what makes the difference between them? I have in my pocket a button which I ripped off the coat of the Marquis of Ossoli on the sea-shore the other day. Held up it intercepts the light—an actual button—and yet all the life it is connected with is less substantial to me, and interests me less, than my faintest dream. Our thoughts are the epochs in our lives, all else is but as a journal of the winds that blew while we were here.

I say to myself— Do a little more of that work which you have confessed to be good. You are neither satisfied nor dissatisfied with yourself without reason. Have you not a thinking-faculty of inestimable value? If there is an experiment which you would like to try—try it. Do not entertain doubts if they are not agreeable to you. Remember that you need not eat unless you are hungry. Do not read the newspapers. Improve every opportunity to be melancholy. As for health, consider yourself well. Do not engage to find things as you think they are. Do what nobody else can do for you— Omit to do anything else.

It is not easy to make our lives respectable by any course of activity— We have repeatedly to withdraw into our shells of thought, like the tortoise, somewhat helplessly; yet there is more than philosophy in that.

Do not waste any reverence on my attitude. I merely manage to sit up where I have dropped. I am sure that my acquaintances mistake me. They ask my advice on high matters, but they do not know, even how poorly on't I am for hats & shoes. I have hardly a shift. Just as shabby as I am in my outward apparel, aye, and more lamentably shabby—am I in my inward substance. If I should turn myself inside out, my rags and meanness would indeed appear. I am something to him that made me undoubtedly, but not much to any other that he has made.

Would it not be worth the while to discover Nature in Milton—be native to the universe? I too love Concord best; but I am glad when I discover in oceans and wildernesses far away the materials of a million Concords; indeed I am lost unless I discover them.[1] I see less difference between a city and a swamp than formerly. It is a swamp however, too dismal[2] and dreary even for me, and I should be glad if there were fewer owls & frogs & mosquitoes in it. I prefer even a more cultivated place—free from miasma and crocodiles— I am so sophisticated—and I will take my choice.

As for missing friends—what if we do miss one another— have we not agreed on a rendezvous? While each wanders his own way through the wood, without anxiety, aye with serene joy, though it be on his hands & knees over rocks and fallen trees,[3] he cannot but be on the right way.— There is no wrong way to him. How can he be said to miss his friends, whom the fruits still nourish and the elements sustain? A man who missed his friends at a turn, went on buoyantly, dividing the friendly air, & humming a tune to himself, ever and anon kneeling with delight to study each little lichen in his path, and scarcely made three miles a day for friendship.

As for conforming outwardly, and living your own life inwardly,—I do not think much of that. Let not your right hand know what your left hand does[4] in that line of business. It will prove a failure. Just as successfully can you walk against a sharp steel edge which divides you cleanly right and left.[5] Do you wish to try your ability to resist distension? It is a greater strain than any soul can long endure. When you get God to pulling one way and the Devil the other, each having his feet well braced,—to say nothing of the conscience sawing transversely—almost any timber will give way.

I do not dare invite you earnestly to come to Concord, because I know too well that the berries are not thick in my field, and we should have to take it out in viewing the landscape. But come on every account, and we will see—one another.

Henry D. Thoreau

✒ Letter Ten

July 21, 1852, Wednesday; Concord, Massachusetts

A great deal had occurred in the two years since Thoreau's last letter. He and Channing had traveled to Montreal and Quebec in the fall of 1850, an excursion which Thoreau wrote up and lectured on in December 1851, one of fourteen lectures he had delivered since his last letter. The sectional strife that would tear the country apart in less than a decade accelerated dramatically with the passage of the Compromise of 1850, the most contentious part of which was the Fugitive Slave Law. This component of the omnibus bill mandated federal resources for the remanding of escaped slaves, but Americans at this time were highly skeptical of provisions allowing the federal government to infringe upon a state's sovereignty by forcibly removing anyone from within the state's borders. The April 1851 rendition of Anthony Sims from Boston ignited the wrath of Northerners, driving many into antislavery ranks. Thoreau himself responded by stepping up his participation in the Underground Railroad, sheltering escaped slaves and helping them on their way to Canada. He delivered the earliest version of his "Walking" lecture in April 1851, prefacing the lecture with a caustic remark about the Fugitive Slave Law. In this lecture he first uttered what may be his most famous proclamation, "[I]n Wildness is the preservation of the world." Later he would note that he regarded this lecture as "a sort of introduction to all I may write hereafter," a reference to the large natural history projects he would take up later in the decade and would continue working on for the remainder of his life. At the end of the following month, May 1851, after being fitted with false teeth, he delivered the lecture in Worcester, staying on three days to visit with Blake, Brown, and his other Worcester friends. His surveying business had been keeping him busier than he wished, although he continued to need the money to pay down his debt for *A Week*. Late in 1851 he finally got back to work on his *Walden* manuscript and would continue to steadily refine it until publication in August 1854. Since the fall of 1850 or so he had been putting considerable effort into learning botany, and studying the woods and fields of his hometown more systematically. At the time of this letter he was particularly interested in tracking the seasons more carefully, as the first note for this letter indicates. Blake was by this time once again back in Worcester after having taught in Boston during the fall of 1851 and perhaps into the spring of 1852.

Concord July 21st '52.

Mr Blake,

I am too stupidly well these days to write to you. My life is almost altogether outward,[1] all shell and no tender kernel; so that I fear the report of it would be only a nut for you to crack, with no meat in it for you to eat. Moreover, you have not cornered me up, and I enjoy such large liberty in writing to you that I feel as vague as the air. However, I rejoice to hear that you have attended so patiently to anything which I have said heretofore, and have detected any truths in it. It encourages me to say more—not in this letter I fear—but in some book which I may write one day. I am glad to know that I am as much to any mortal as a persistent and *con*sistent scarecrow is to a farmer—such a bundle of straw in a man's clothing as I am—with a few bits of tin to sparkle in the sun[2] dangling about me. As if I were hard at work there in the field. However, if this kind of life saves any man's corn,—why he is the gainer. I am not afraid that you will flatter me as long as you know what I am, as well as what I think, or aim to be, & distinguish between these two, for then it will commonly happen that if you praise the last, you will condemn the first.

I remember that walk to Asnebumskit[3] very well;—a fit place to go on a Sunday, one of the true temples of the earth. A temple you know was anciently "an open place without a roof,"[4] whose walls served merely to shut out the world, and direct the mind toward heaven; but a modern *meeting house* shuts out the heavens, while it crowds the world into still closer quarters. Best of all is it when as on a *Mt.* top you have for all walls your own elevations and deeps of surrounding ether. The partridge berries watered with *Mt.* dews, which are gathered there, are more memorable to me than the words which I last heard from the pulpit at least, and for my part I would rather walk toward Rutland[5] than Jerusalem. Rutland—modern town—land of ruts—trivial and worn—not too sacred—with no holy sepulchre, but prophane green fields and dusty roads,—and opportunity to live as holy a life as you can;—where the sacredness if there is any is all in yourself and not in the place.

I fear that your Worcester people do not often enough go to the hilltops, though, as I am told, the springs lie nearer to the surface on your hills than in your valleys.[6] They have the reputation of being Free Soilers[7]— Do they insist on a free atmosphere too, that is, on freedom for the head or brain as well as the feet? If I were consciously to join any party it would be that which is the most free to entertain thought.

All the world complain now a days of a press of trivial duties & engagements which prevents their employing themselves on some higher ground they know of,—but undoubtedly if they were made of the right stuff to work on that higher ground, provided they were released from all those engagements—they would now at once fulfill the superior engagement, and neglect all the rest, as naturally as they breathe. They would never be caught saying that they had no time for this when the dullest man knows that this is all that he has time for. No man who acts from a sense of duty ever puts the lesser duty above the greater. No man has the desire and the ability to work on high things but he has also the ability to build himself a high staging.

As for passing *through* any great and glorious experience, and rising *above* it,—as an eagle might fly athwart the evening sky to rise into still brighter & fairer regions of the heavens, I cannot say that I ever sailed so creditably, but my bark ever seemed thwarted by some side wind and went off over the edge and now only occasionally tacks back toward the center of that sea again. I have outgrown nothing good, but, I do not fear to say, fallen behind by whole continents of virtue which should have been passed as islands in my course; but I trust—what else can I trust?—that with a stiff wind some Friday, when I have thrown some of my cargo over board, I may make up for all that distance lost.

Perchance the time will come when we shall not be content to go back & forth upon a raft to some huge Homeric or Shak-spearean India-man[8] that lies upon the reef, but build a bark out of that wreck, and others that are buried in the sands of this desolate island, and such new timber as may be required, in which to sail away to whole new worlds of light & life where our friends are.

Write again. There is one respect in which you did not finish your letter, you did not write it with ink, and it is not so good therefore against or for you in the eye of the law,[9] nor in the eye of

H. D. T.

🖎 *Letter Eleven*

[September 1852; Concord, Massachusetts]

In July 1852, Blake and one of his longtime students, Nancy Pope Howe Conant (1829–1872), decided they would marry during the forthcoming autumn. At thirty-six years of age, Blake had been a widower and single parent for six years. His fiancée was thirteen years his junior and from a wealthy family in Sterling, a small town twelve miles north of downtown Worcester. The couple married at a Unitarian church in Sterling on October 27, 1852. The marriage brought Blake financial security—a Worcester newspaper two years later reported that he paid tax on $20,590, whereas before he had been struggling to make ends meet—but more importantly it allied him to a woman who seems to have been as high-minded as he was. In late August 1852 he wrote to both Thoreau and Amos Bronson Alcott asking them, as he wrote in his letter to Alcott, how they thought a man and a woman could "help each other to be more truly solitary in the good & beautiful sense, to be more truly free, to be nearer the common Friend that we could be, apart? For we aim, I think, at nothing less than that. How shall we treat each other, with what reserve, with what Holy Reverence, so that the Mystery, the Poetry, & Beauty which hang about the dawning of love, may not be changed by too close an intercourse, by sharing, in common, the cares of daily life, into a prosaic & vulgar familiarity." His letter makes clear that he had conferred with his fiancée on these matters. Clearly, then, the high moral purpose of marital union was suggested by Blake and his fiancée just as much as it was assumed by Thoreau. Although Thoreau's cover letter for the two enclosures is undated, he would probably have needed two or three weeks to gather the "disconnected fragments" on "Love" and "Chastity and Sensuality" from his journal. Probably he sent them during September 1852. Just two passages from "Love" are extant in his early journal, the passages dating from the late summer and early autumn of 1849; all the other passages making up the two enclosures were probably torn out of the manuscript notebooks during the writing process. Reading these enclosures containing materials from 1849 within the context of Thoreau's letters of 1852 gives one a clear sense of how dramatically his interests and prose style had changed during that three-year period.

Mr. Blake,

Here come the sentences which I promised you. You may keep them if you will regard & use them as the disconnected fragments of what I may find to be a completer essay, on looking over my journal at last, and may claim again.

I send you the thoughts on chastity & sensuality with diffidence and shame, not knowing how far I speak to the condition of men generally, or how far I betray my peculiar defects. Pray enlighten me on this point if you can.

Henry D. Thoreau

∽ *Letter Eleven, Enclosure 1*
[September 1852; Concord, Massachusetts]

LOVE.

What the essential difference between man and woman is that they should be thus attracted to one another, no one has satisfactorily answered. Perhaps we must acknowledge the justness of the distinction which assigns to man the sphere of wisdom, and to woman that of love, though neither belongs exclusively to either. Man is continually saying to woman, Why will you not be more wise? Woman is continually saying to man, Why will you not be more loving? It is not in their wills to be wise or to be loving; but, unless each is both wise and loving, there can be neither wisdom nor love.

All transcendent goodness is one, though appreciated in different ways, or by different senses. In beauty we see it, in music we hear it, in fragrance we scent it, in the palatable the pure palate tastes it, and in rare health the whole body feels it. The variety is in the surface or manifestation; but the radical identity we fail to express. The lover sees in the glance of his beloved the same beauty that in the sunset paints the western skies. It is the same daimon, here lurking under a human eyelid, and there under the closing eyelids of the day. Here, in small compass, is the ancient and natural beauty of evening and morning. What loving astronomer has ever fathomed the ethereal depths of the eye?

The maiden conceals a fairer flower and sweeter fruit than any calyx in the field, and if she goes with averted face confiding in her purity and high resolves, she will make the heavens retrospective, and all nature humbly confess its queen.

Under the influence of this sentiment man is a string of an aeolian harp,[1] which vibrates with the zephyrs of the eternal morning.

There is at first thought something trivial in the commonness of love. So many Indian youths and maidens along these banks have in ages past yielded to the influence of this great civilizer. Nevertheless this generation is not disgusted nor discouraged, for Love is no individual's experience, and though we are imperfect mediums, it does not partake of our imperfection; though we are finite, it is infinite and eternal, and the same divine influence broods over these banks, whatever race may inhabit them, and perchance still would, even if the human race did not dwell here.

Perhaps an instinct survives through the intensest actual love, which prevents entire abandonment and devotion, and makes the most ardent lover a little reserved. It is the anticipation of change. For the most ardent lover is not the less practically wise, and seeks a love which will last forever.

Considering how few poetical Friendships there are, it is remarkable that so many are married. It would seem as if men yielded too easy an obedience to nature without consulting their genius. One may be drunk with love without being any nearer to finding his mate. There is more of good nature than of good sense at the bottom of most marriages. But the good nature must have the counsel of the good Spirit or Intelligence. If common sense had been consulted how many marriages would never have taken place; if uncommon or divine sense, how few marriages such as we witness, would ever have taken place!

Our love may be ascending or descending. What is its character if it may be said of it—

> We must *respect* the souls above,
> But only *those below* we *love*.[2]

Love is a severe critic. Hate can pardon more than Love. They who aspire to love worthily subject themselves to an ordeal more rigid than any other.

Is your friend such a one that an increase of worth on your part will surely make her more your friend? Is she retained, is she attracted, by more nobleness in you, by more of that virtue which is peculiarly yours, or is she indifferent and blind to that? Is she to be flattered and won by your meeting her on any other than the ascending path? Then duty requires that you separate from her.

Love must be as much a light as a flame.

Where there is not discernment, the behavior even of the purest soul may in effect amount to coarseness.

A man of fine perceptions is more truly feminine than a merely sentimental woman. The heart is blind; but Love is not blind. None of the gods is so discriminating.

In love and friendship the imagination is as much exercised as the heart; and if either is outraged the other will be estranged. It is commonly the imagination which is wounded first, rather than the heart,—it is so much the more sensitive.

Comparatively, we can excuse any offence against the heart, but not against the imagination. The imagination knows—nothing escapes its glance from out its eyry—and it controls the breast. My heart may still yearn toward the valley, but my imagination will not permit me to jump off the precipice that debars me from it, for it is wounded, its wings are clipt, and it cannot fly, even descendingly. Our "blundering hearts!" some poet says.[3] The imagination never forgets, it is a re-membering. It is not foundationless, but most reasonable, and it alone uses all the knowledge of the intellect.

Love is the profoundest of secrets. Divulged, even to the beloved, it is no longer Love. As if it were merely I that loved you. When love ceases, then it is divulged.

In our intercourse with one we love, we wish to have answered those questions at the end of which we do not raise our voice; against which we put no interrogation-mark,—answered with the same unfailing, universal aim toward every point of the compass.

I require that thou knowest everything without being told anything. I parted from my beloved because there was one thing which I had to tell her. She *questioned* me. She should have known all by sympathy. That I had to tell it her was the difference between us,—the misunderstanding.

A lover never hears anything that is *told*, for that is commonly either false or stale; but he hears things taking place, as the sentinels heard Trenck mining in the ground, and thought it was moles.[4]

The relation may be profaned in many ways. The parties may not regard it with equal sacredness. What if the lover should learn that his beloved dealt in incantations and philters! What if he should hear that she consulted a clairvoyant! The spell would be instantly broken.

If to chaffer and higgle are bad in trade, they are much worse in Love. It demands directness as of an arrow.

There is danger that we lose sight of what our friend is absolutely, while considering what she is to us alone.

The lover wants no partiality. He says, Be so kind as to be just.

> Canst thou love with thy mind,
>   And reason with thy heart?
> Canst thou be kind,
>   And from thy darling part?
>
> Canst thou range earth, sea, and air,
>   And so meet me everywhere?
> Through all events I will pursue thee,
>   Through all persons I will woo thee.[5]

I need thy hate as much as thy love. Thou wilt not repel me entirely when thou repellest what is evil in me.

> Indeed, indeed, I cannot tell,
> Though I ponder on it well,
> Which were easier to state,
> All my love or all my hate.
> Surely, surely, thou wilt trust me
> When I say thou dost disgust me.
> O I hate thee with a hate
> That would fain annihilate;
> Yet, sometimes, against my will,

My dear Friend, I love thee still.
It were treason to our love,
And a sin to God above,
One iota to abate
Of a pure, impartial hate.[6]

It is not enough that we are truthful; we must cherish and carry out high purposes to be truthful about.

It must be rare, indeed, that we meet with one to whom we are prepared to be quite ideally related, as she to us. We should have no reserve; we should give the whole of ourselves to that society; we should have no duty aside from that. One who could bear to be so wonderfully and beautifully exaggerated every day. I would take my friend out of her low self and set her higher, infinitely higher, and *there* know her. But, commonly, men are as much afraid of love as of hate. They have lower engagements. They have near ends to serve. They have not imagination enough to be thus employed about a human being, but must be coopering a barrel, forsooth.

What a difference, whether, in all your walks, you meet only strangers, or in one house is one who knows you, and whom you know. To have a brother or a sister! To have a gold mine on your farm! To find diamonds in the gravel heaps before your door! How rare these things are! To share the day with you,— to people the earth. Whether to have a god or a goddess for companion in your walks, or to walk alone with hinds and villains and carles.[7] Would not a friend enhance the beauty of the landscape as much as a deer or hare? Everything would acknowledge and serve such a relation; the corn in the field, and the cranberries in the meadow. The flowers would bloom, and the birds sing, with a new impulse. There would be more fair days in the year.

The object of love expands and grows before us to eternity, until it includes all that is lovely, and we become all that can love.

~ *Letter Eleven, Enclosure 2*
[September 1852; Concord, Massachusetts]

CHASTITY AND SENSUALITY.

The subject of sex is a remarkable one, since, though its phenomena concern us so much, both directly and indirectly, and, sooner or later, it occupies the thoughts of all, yet all mankind, as it were, agree to be silent about it, at least the sexes commonly one to another. One of the most interesting of all human facts is veiled more completely than any mystery. It is treated with such secrecy and awe, as surely do not go to any religion. I believe that it is unusual even for the most intimate friends to communicate the pleasures and anxieties connected with this fact, much as the external affair of love, its comings and goings, are bruited. The Shakers[1] do not exaggerate it so much by their manner of speaking of it, as all mankind by their manner of keeping silence about it. Not that men should speak on this or any subject without having any thing worthy to say; but it is plain that the education of man has hardly commenced,—there is so little genuine intercommunication.

In a pure society, the subject of copulation[2] would not be so often avoided from shame and not from reverence, winked out of sight, and hinted at only, but treated naturally and simply,—perhaps simply avoided, like the kindred mysteries. If it cannot be spoken of for shame, how can it be acted of? But, doubtless, there is far more purity, as well as more impurity, than is apparent.

Men commonly couple with their idea of marriage a slight

degree at least of sensuality; but every lover, the world over, believes in its inconceivable purity.

If it is the result of a pure love, there can be nothing sensual in marriage. Chastity is something positive, not negative. It is the virtue of the married especially. All lusts or base pleasures must give place to loftier delights. They who meet as superior beings cannot perform the deeds of inferior ones. The deeds of love are less questionable than any action of an individual can be, for, it being founded on the rarest mutual respect, the parties incessantly stimulate each other to a loftier and purer life, and the act in which they are associated must be pure and noble indeed, for innocence and purity can have no equal. In this relation we deal with one whom we respect more religiously even than we respect our better selves, and we shall necessarily conduct as in the presence of God. What presence can be more awful to the lover than that of his beloved?

If you seek the warmth even of affection from a similar motive to that from which cats and dogs and slothful persons hug the fire, because your temperature is low through sloth, you are on the downward road, and it is but to plunge yet deeper into sloth. Better the cold affection of the sun, reflected from fields of ice and snow, or his warmth in some still wintry dell. The warmth of celestial love does not relax, but nerves and braces its enjoyer. Warm your body by healthful exercise, not by cowering over a stove. Warm your spirit by performing independently noble deeds, not by ignobly seeking the sympathy of your fellows who are no better than yourself. A man's social and spiritual discipline must answer to his corporeal. He must lean on a friend who has a hard breast, as he would lie on a hard bed.

He must drink cold water for his only beverage. So he must not hear sweetened and colored words, but pure and refreshing truths. He must daily bathe in truth cold as spring water, not warmed by the sympathy of friends.

Can love be in aught allied to dissipation? Let us love by refusing, not accepting one another. Love and lust are far asunder. The one is good, the other bad. When the affectionate sympathize by their higher natures, there is love; but there is danger that they will sympathize by their lower natures, and then there is lust. It is not necessary that this be deliberate, hardly even conscious; but, in the close contact of affection, there is danger that we may stain and pollute one another, for we cannot embrace but with an entire embrace.

We must love our friend so much that she shall be associated with our purest and holiest thoughts alone. When there is impurity, we have "descended to meet,"[3] though we knew it not.

The *luxury* of affection,—there's the danger. There must be some nerve and heroism in our love, as of a winter morning. In the religion of all nations a purity is hinted at, which, I fear, men never attain to. We may love and not elevate one another. The love that takes us as it finds us degrades us. What watch we must keep over the fairest and purest of our affections, lest there be some taint about them. May we so love as never to have occasion to repent of our love.

There is to be attributed to sensuality the loss to language of how many pregnant symbols? Flowers, which, by their infinite hues and fragrance, celebrate the marriage of the plants, are intended for a symbol of the open and unsuspected beauty of all true marriage, when man's flowering season arrives.

Virginity, too, is a budding flower, and by an impure marriage the virgin is deflowered. Whoever loves flowers, loves virgins and chastity. Love and lust are as far asunder as a flower garden is from a brothel.

J. Biberg, in the *Amœnitates Botanicæ*, edited by Linnæus, observes (I translate from the Latin): "The organs of generation, which, in the animal kingdom, are for the most part concealed by nature as if they were to be ashamed of, in the vegetable kingdom are exposed to the eyes of all; and, when the nuptials of plants are celebrated, it is wonderful what delight they afford to the beholder, refreshing the senses with the most agreeable color and the sweetest odor; and, at the same time, bees and other insects, not to mention the humming-bird, extract honey from their nectaries, and gather wax from their effete pollen."[4] Linnæus himself calls the calyx the *thalamus,* or bridal chamber; and the corolla the *aulaeum,* or tapestry of it, and proceeds to explain thus every part of the flower.[5]

Who knows but evil spirits might corrupt the flowers themselves, rob them of their fragrance and their fair hues, and turn their marriage into a secret shame and defilement? Already they are of various qualities, and there is one whose nuptials fill the lowlands in June with the odor of carrion.

The intercourse of the sexes, I have dreamed, is incredibly beautiful, too fair to be remembered. I have had thoughts about it, but they are among the most fleeting and irrecoverable in my experience. It is strange that men will talk of miracles, revelation, inspiration, and the like, as things past, while love remains.

A true marriage will differ in no wise from illumination. In all perception of the truth there is a divine ecstasy, an inexpressible delirium of joy, as when a youth embraces his betrothed virgin. The ultimate delights of a true marriage are one with this.

No wonder that, out of such a union, not as end, but as accompaniment, comes the undying race of man. The womb is a most fertile soil.

Some have asked if the stock of men could not be improved,—if they could not be bred as cattle. Let Love be purified, and all the rest will follow. A pure love is thus, indeed, the panacea for all the ills of the world.

The only excuse for reproduction is improvement. Nature abhors repetition. Beasts merely propagate their kind; but the offspring of noble men and women will be superior to themselves, as their aspirations are. By their fruits ye shall know them.[6]

🌿 *Letter Twelve*

February 27, 1853, Sunday; Concord, Massachusetts

The essay versions of Thoreau's "An Excursion to Canada" lectures began to appear serially in the new *Putnam's Monthly Magazine of American Literature, Science, and Art* in January 1853 but publication was halted after the third installment (March) because Thoreau refused to allow George William Curtis (1824–1892), the editor, to remove certain passages he regarded as "heresies." Still needing to pay down his debt for *A Week,* Thoreau stayed busy surveying, as he mentions at the beginning of this letter. He had delivered no lectures during the preceding nine months and would not deliver another till December. He continued work on his *Walden* manuscript and continued extracting passages from the books he was reading into his notebooks on Indians and natural history.

Concord Feb. 27 '53

Mr Blake,

I have not answered your letter before because I have been almost constantly in the fields surveying[1] of late. It is long since I have spent so many days so profitably in a pecuniary sense; so unprofitably, it seems to me, in a more important sense. I have earned just a dollar a day for 76 days past;[2] for though I charge at a higher rate for the days which are seen to be spent, yet so many more are spent than appears. This is instead of lecturing, which has not offered to pay for that book which I printed.[3] I have not only cheap hours, but cheap weeks and months, i.e. weeks which are bought at the rate I have named. Not that they are quite lost to me, or make me very melancholy, alas! for I too often take a cheap satisfaction in so spending them,—weeks of pasturing and browsing, like beeves and deer, which give me animal health, it may be, but create a tough skin over the soul and intellectual part. Yet if men should offer my body a maintenance for the work of my head alone, I feel that it would be a dangerous temptation.

As to whether what you speak of as the "world's way" (which for the most part is my way) or that which is shown me, is the better, the former is imposture, the latter is truth. I have the coldest confidence in the last. There is only such hesitation as the appetites feel in following the aspirations. The clod hesitates because it is inert, wants *animation*.[4] The one is the way of death, the other of life everlasting. My hours are not "cheap in such a way that *I* doubt whether the world's way would not have been better," but cheap in such a way, that I doubt whether the world's way, which I have adopted for the time, could be worse. The whole enterprise of this nation which is not an upward, but a westward one, toward Oregon California, Japan &c, is totally devoid of interest to me, whether performed on foot or by a Pacific railroad. It is not illustrated by a thought, it is not warmed by a sentiment, there is nothing in it which one should lay down his life for, nor even his gloves, hardly which one should take up a newspaper for. It is perfectly heathenish—a filibustering *toward* heaven by the great western route. No, they may go their way to their manifest destiny[5] which I trust is not mine. May my 76 dollars whenever I get them help to carry me in the other direction. I see them on their winding way, but no music "is" wafted from their host, only the rattling of change in their pockets. I would rather be a captive, knight,[6] and let them all pass by, than be free only to go whither they are bound. What end do they propose to themselves beyond Japan?[7] What aims more lofty have they than the prairie dogs?

As it respects these things I have not changed an opinion one iota from the first. As the stars looked to me when I was a shepherd in Assyria[8] they look to me now a New Englander. The higher the *mt.* on which you stand, the less change in the prospect from year to year, from age to age. Above a certain height, there is no change. I am a Switzer on the edge of the glacier, with his advantages & disadvantages, goitre, or what not. (You may suspect it to be some kind of swelling at any rate.) I have had but one *spiritual* birth (excuse the word,) and now whether it rains or snows, whether I laugh or cry, fall farther below or approach nearer to my standard, whether Pierce or Scott[9] is elected,—not a new scintillation of light flashes on me, but ever and anon, though with longer intervals, the same surprising & everlastingly new light dawns to me, with only such variations as in the coming of the natural day, with which indeed, it is often coincident.

As to how to preserve potatoes from rotting, your opinion may change from year to year, but as to how to preserve your soul from rotting, I have nothing to learn but something to practise.

Thus I declaim against them, but I in my folly am the world I condemn.

I very rarely indeed, if ever, "feel any itching to be what is called useful to my fellowmen." Sometimes, it may be when my thoughts for want of employment, fall into a beaten path or humdrum, I have dreamed idly of stopping a man's horse that was running away, but perchance I wished that he might run in order that I might stop him,—or, of putting out a fire, but then of course it must have got well a-going. Now, to tell the truth, I do not dream much of acting upon horses before they run, or of preventing fires which are not yet kindled. What a foul subject is this, of doing good,[10] instead of minding one's life, which should be his business—doing good as a dead carcass, which is only fit for manure, instead of as a living man,—instead of taking care to flourish & smell & taste sweet and refresh all mankind to the extent of our capacity & quality. People will sometimes try to persuade you that you have done something from that motive, as if you did not already know enough about it. If I ever *did* a man any good, in their sense, of course it was something exceptional, and insignificant compared with the good or evil which I am constantly doing by being what I am. As if you were to preach to ice to shape itself into burning glasses,[11] which are sometimes useful, and so the peculiar properties of ice be lost— Ice that merely performs the office of a burning glass does not do its duty.

The problem of life becomes one cannot say by how many degrees more complicated as our material wealth is increased, whether that needle they tell of[12] was a gate-way or not,—since the problem is not merely nor mainly to get life for our bodies, but by this or a similar discipline to get life for our souls; by cultivating the lowland farm on right principles, that is with this view, to turn it into an upland farm. You have so many more talents to account for.[13] If I accomplish as much more in spiritual work as I am richer in worldly goods, then I am just as worthy, or worth just as much as I was before, and no more. I see that, in my own case, money *might* be of great service to me, but probably it would not be, for the difficulty ever is that I do not improve my opportunities, and therefore I am not prepared to have my opportunities increased. Now I warn you, if it be as you say, you have got to put on the pack of an Upland Farmer in good earnest the coming spring, the lowland farm being cared for, aye you must be selecting your seeds forthwith and doing what winter work you can; and while others are raising potatoes and Baldwin apples for you, you must be raising apples of the Hesperides[14] for them. (Only hear how he preaches!) No man can suspect that he is the proprietor of an Upland farm, upland in the sense that it will produce nobler crops and better repay cultivation in the long run, but he will be perfectly sure that he ought to cultivate it.

Though we are desirous to earn our bread, we need not be anxious to *satisfy* men for it—though we shall take care to pay them, but God[15] who alone gave it to us. Men may in effect put us in the debtor's jail, for that matter, simply for paying our whole debt to God which includes our debt to them, and though we have his receipt for it, for his paper is dishonored. The carrier will tell you that he has no stock in his bank.

How prompt we are to satisfy the hunger & thirst of our bodies; how slow to satisfy the hunger & thirst of our *souls*. Indeed we who would be practical folks cannot use this word without blushing because of our infidelity, having starved this substance almost to a shadow. We feel it to be as absurd as if a man were to break forth into a eulogy on *his dog* who hasn't any. An ordinary man will work every day for a year at shovelling dirt to support his body, or a family of bodies, but he is an extraordinary man who will work a whole day in a year for the support of his soul. Even the priests, the men of God, so called, for the most part confess that they work for the support of the body. But he alone is the truly enterprising & practical man who succeeds in *maintaining* his soul here. Haven't we our everlasting life to get? And isn't that the only excuse at last for eating drinking sleeping or even carrying an umbrella when it rains? A man might as well devote himself to raising pork, as to fattening the bodies or temporal part merely of the whole human family. If we made the true distinction we should almost all of us be seen to be in the almshouse for souls.

I am much indebted to you because you look so steadily at the better side, or rather the true center of me (for our true center may & perhaps oftenest does lie entirely aside from us, and we are in fact eccentric,) and as I have elsewhere said "Give me an opportunity to live."[16] You speak as if the image or idea which I see were reflected from me to you, and I see it again reflected from you to me, because we stand at the right angle to one another; and so it goes, zig-zag, to what successive reflecting surfaces, before it is all dissipated, or absorbed by the more unreflecting, or differently reflecting,—who knows? Or perhaps what you see directly you refer to me. What a little shelf is required, by which we may impinge upon another, and build there our eyrie in the clouds, and all the heavens we see above us we refer to the crags around and beneath us. Some piece of mica, as it were, in the face or eyes of one, as on the Delectable *Mts.,*[17] slanted at the right angle, reflects the heavens to us. But in the slow geological depressions & upheavals, these mutual angles are disturbed, these suns set & new ones rise to us. That ideal which I worshipped was a greater stranger to the mica than to me. It was not the hero I admired but the reflection from his epaulet or helmet. It is nothing (for us) permanently inherent in another, but his attitude or relation to what we prize that we admire. The meanest man may glitter with micacious particles to his fellow's eye. There are the spangles that adorn a man. The highest union—the only *un*-ion[18] (don't laugh) or central oneness, is the coincidence of visual rays. Our club room was an apartment in a constellation where our visual rays met (and there was no debate about the restaurant). The way between us is over the mount.

Your words make me think of a man of my acquaintance whom I occasionally meet, whom you too appear to have met, one Myself, as he is called. Yet why not call him *Your*-self? If you have met with him & know him it is all I have done, and surely where there is a mutual acquaintance the my & thy make a distinction without a difference.

I do not wonder that you do not like my Canada story.[19] It concerns me but little, and probably is not worth the time it took to tell it. Yet I had absolutely no design whatever in my mind, but simply to report what I saw. I have inserted all of myself that was implicated or made the excursion. It has come to an end at any rate, they will print no more, but return me my mss. when it is but little more than half done—as well as another I had sent them, because the editor Curtis requires the liberty to omit the heresies without consulting me—a privilege California is not rich enough to bid for.[20]

I thank you again & again for attending to me; that is to say I am glad that you hear me and that you also are glad. Hold fast to your most indefinite waking dream. The very green dust on the walls is an organized vegetable; the atmosphere has its fauna & flora floating in it; & shall we think that dreams are but dust & ashes, are always disintegrated & crumbling thoughts and not dust like thoughts trooping to its standard with music systems beginning to be organized. These expectations these are roots these are nuts which even the poorest man has in his bin, and roasts or cracks them occasionally in winter evenings, which even the poor debtor retains with his bed and his pig, i.e. his idleness & sensuality. Men go to the opera because they hear there a faint expression in sound of this news which is never quite distinctly proclaimed. Suppose a man were to sell the hue the least amount of coloring matter in the superficies of his thought,—for a farm—were to exchange an absolute & infinite value for a relative & finite one—to gain the whole world & lose his own soul![21]

Do not wait as long as I have before you write. If you will look at another star I will try to supply my side of the triangle.

Tell Mr Brown that I remember him & trust that he remembers me.

Yrs

H.D.T.

P.S. Excuse this rather flippant preaching—which does not cost me enough—and do not think that I mean you *always*—though your letter *requested* the subjects.

✍ Letter Thirteen

April 10, 1853, Sunday; Concord, Massachusetts

Concord, April 10, 1853.

Mr. Blake,—

Another singular kind of spiritual foot-ball,—really name-less, handleless, homeless, like myself,—a mere arena for thoughts and feelings; definite enough outwardly, indefinite more than enough inwardly. But I do not know why we should be styled "misters" or "masters": we come so near to being any-thing or nothing, and seeing that we are mastered, and not wholly sorry to be mastered, by the least phenomenon. It seems to me that we are the mere creatures of thought,—one of the lowest forms of intellectual life, we men,—as the sunfish is of animal life.[1] As yet our thoughts have acquired no definiteness nor solidity; they are purely molluscous, not vertebrate; and the height of our existence is to float upward in an ocean where the sun shines,—appearing only like a vast soup or chowder to the eyes of the immortal navigators. It is wonderful that I can be here, and you there, and that we can correspond, and do many other things, when, in fact, there is so little of us, either or both, anywhere. In a few minutes, I expect, this slight film or dash of vapor that I am will be what is called asleep,—resting! forsooth from what? Hard work? and thought? The hard work of the dandelion down, which floats over the meadow all day; the hard work of a pismire that labors to raise a hillock all day, and even by moonlight. Suddenly I can come forward into the utmost apparent distinctness, and speak with a sort of emphasis to you; and the next moment I am so faint an entity, and make so slight an impression, that nobody can find the traces of me. I try to hunt myself up, and find the little of me that is discoverable is falling asleep, and then I assist and tuck it up. It is getting late. How can *I* starve or feed? Can *I* be said to sleep? There is not enough of me even for that. If you hear a noise,— 't aint I,—'t aint I,—as the dog says with a tin-kettle tied to his tail.[2] I read of something happening to another the other day: how happens it that nothing ever happens to me? A dandelion down that never alights,—settles,—blown off by a boy to see if his mother wanted him,[3]—some divine boy in the upper pastures.

Well, if there really is another such a meteor[4] sojourning in these spaces, I would like to ask you if you know whose estate this is that we are on? For my part I enjoy it well enough, what with the wild apples and the scenery; but I shouldn't wonder if the owner set his dog on me next. I could remember something not much to the purpose, probably; but if I stick to what I do know, then—

It is worth the while to live respectably unto ourselves. We can possibly *get along* with a neighbor, even with a bedfellow, whom we respect but very little; but as soon as it comes to this, that we do not respect ourselves, then we do not get along at all, no matter how much money we are paid for halting. There are old heads in the world who cannot help me by their example or advice to live worthily and satisfactorily to myself; but I believe that it is in my power to elevate myself this very hour above the common level of my life. It is better to have your head in the clouds, and know where you are, if indeed you cannot get it above them, than to breathe the clearer atmosphere below them, and think that you are in paradise.

Once you were in Milton doubting what to do. To live a better life—this surely can be done. Dot and carry one.[5] Wait not for a clear sight, for that you are to get. What you see clearly you may omit to do. Milton and Worcester? It is all Blake, Blake. Never mind the rats in the wall; the cat will take care of them. All that men have said or are is a very faint rumor, and it is not worth the while to remember or refer to that. If you are to meet God, will you refer to anybody out of that court? How shall men know how I succeed, unless they are in at the life? I did not see the "Times" reporter there.

Is it not delightful to provide one's self with the necessaries of life,—to collect dry wood for the fire when the weather grows cool, or fruits when we grow hungry?—not till then. And then we have all the time left for thought!

Of what use were it, pray, to get a little wood to burn, to warm your body this cold weather, if there were not a divine fire kindled at the same time to warm your spirit?

"Unless above himself he can
Erect himself, how poor a thing is man!"[6]

I cuddle up by my stove, and there I get up another fire which warms fire itself. Life is so short that it is not wise to take roundabout ways, nor can we spend much time in waiting. Is it absolutely necessary, then, that we should do as we are doing? Are we chiefly under obligations to the devil, like Tom Walker?[7] Though it is late to leave off this wrong way, it will seem early the moment we begin in the right way; instead of mid-afternoon, it will be early morning with us. We have not got half way to dawn yet.[8]

As for the lectures, I feel that I have something to say, especially on Traveling, Vagueness, and Poverty; but I cannot come now. I will wait till I am fuller, and have fewer engagements. Your suggestions will help me much to write them when I am ready. I am going to Haverhill tomorrow, surveying, for a week or more. You met me on my last errand thither.[9]

I trust that you realize what an exaggerater[10] I am,—that I lay myself out to exaggerate whenever I have an opportunity,— pile Pelion upon Ossa, to reach heaven so.[11] Expect no trivial truth from me, unless I am on the witness-stand. I will come as near to lying as you can drive a coach-and-four.[12] If it isn't thus and so with me, it is with something. I am not particular whether I get the shells or meat, in view of the latter's worth.

I see that I have not at all answered your letter, but there is time enough for that.

⁊⁊ Letter Fourteen

December 19 and 22, 1853, Monday and Thursday;
Concord, Massachusetts

In September Thoreau had made his second trip into the Maine woods, where he was accompanied by his cousin George Thatcher and the Indian guide Joseph Aitteon. He quickly wrote the excursion up as a lecture and delivered it before his townsmen on December 14. An expanded version of this lecture is the second chapter, "Chesuncook," in his posthumously published book *The Maine Woods.* At the end of October he received the 706 unsold copies of *A Week* (of 1,000 printed), the debt for which he had still not quite paid. Having carried them up two flights of stairs to his attic apartment and observed their vast bulk, he remarked wryly in his journal, "I now have a library of nearly nine hundred volumes, over seven hundred of which I wrote myself." An entry in Emerson's journal of this period appears to relate to this particular letter: "H. D. T. charged Blake, if he could not do hard tasks, to take the soft ones, & when he liked anything, if it was only a picture or a tune, to stay by it, find out what he liked, & draw that sense or meaning out of it, & do *that*: harden it, somehow, & make it his own. Blake thought & thought on this, & wrote afterwards to Henry, that he had got his first glimpse of heaven." Emerson later added the remark, "Henry was a good physician."

Concord, December 19, 1853.

Mr. Blake,—

My debt has accumulated so that I should have answered your last letter at once, if I had not been the subject of what is called a press of engagements, having a lecture to write for last Wednesday, and surveying more than usual besides.[1] It has been a kind of running fight with me,—the enemy not always behind me, I trust.

True, a man cannot lift himself by his own waistbands, because he cannot get out of himself; but he can expand himself (which is better, there being no up nor down in nature), and so split his waistbands, being already within himself.

You speak of doing and being, and the vanity, real or apparent, of much doing. The suckers—I think it is they—make nests in our river in the spring of more than a cart-load of small stones, amid which to deposit their ova.² The other day I opened a muskrat's house.³ It was made of weeds, five feet broad at base, and three feet high, and far and low within it was a little cavity, only a foot in diameter, where the rat dwelt. It may seem trivial, this piling up of weeds, but so the race of muskrats is preserved. We must heap up a great pile of doing, for a small diameter of being. Is it not imperative on us that we *do* something, if we only work in a treadmill? And, indeed, some sort of revolving is necessary to produce a centre and nucleus of being. What exercise is to the body, employment is to the mind and morals. Consider what an amount of drudgery must be performed,—how much humdrum and prosaic labor goes to any work of the least value. There are so many layers of mere white lime in every shell to that thin inner one so beautifully tinted. Let not the shell-fish think to build his house of that alone; and pray, what are its tints to him? Is it not his smooth, close-fitting shirt merely, whose tints *are not* to him, being in the dark, but only when he is gone or dead, and his shell is heaved up to light, a wreck upon the beach, do they appear. With him, too, it is a Song of the Shirt, "Work,—work,—work!"⁴ And the work is not merely a police in the gross sense, but in the higher sense a discipline. If it is surely the means to the highest end we know, can any work be humble or disgusting? Will it not rather be elevating as a ladder, the means by which we are translated?

How admirably the artist is made to accomplish his self-culture by devotion to his art! The wood-sawyer, through his effort to do his work well, becomes not merely a better wood-sawyer, but measurably a better *man*. Few are the men that can work on their navels,—only some Brahmins that I have heard of.[5] To the painter is given some paint and canvas instead; to the Irishman a hog, typical of himself. In a thousand apparently humble ways men busy themselves to make some right take the place of some wrong, if it is only to make a better paste-blacking,— and they are themselves *so much* the better morally for it.

You say that you do not succeed much. Does it concern you enough that you do not? Do you work hard enough at it? Do you get the benefit of discipline out of it? If so, persevere. Is it a more serious thing than to walk a thousand miles in a thousand successive hours? Do you get any corns by it? Do you ever think of hanging yourself on account of failure?

If you are going into that line,—going to besiege the city of God,—you must not only be strong in engines, but prepared with provisions to starve out the garrison. An Irishman came to see me to-day,[6] who is endeavoring to get his family out to this New World. He rises at half past four, milks twenty-eight cows (which has swollen the joints of his fingers), and eats his breakfast, without any milk in his tea or coffee, before six; and so on, day after day, for six and a half dollars a month; and thus he keeps his virtue in him, if he does not add to it; and he regards me as a gentleman able to assist him; but if I ever get to be a gentleman, it will be by working after my fashion harder than he does. If my joints are not swollen, it must be because I deal with the teats of celestial cows before breakfast (and the milker in this case is always allowed some of the milk for his break-fast), to say nothing of the flocks and herds of Admetus[7] after-ward.

It is the art of mankind to polish the world, and everyone who works is scrubbing in some part.

If the work is high and far,

> You must not only aim aright,
> But draw the bow with all your might.[8]

You must qualify yourself to use a bow which no humbler archer can bend.

> "Work,—work,—work!"

Who shall know it for a bow? It is not of yew-tree.[9] It is straighter than a ray of light; flexibility is not known for one of its qualities.

December 22.

So far I had got when I was called off to survey.[10] Pray read the life of Haydon the painter,[11] if you have not. It is a small reve-lation for these latter days; a great satisfaction to know that he has lived, though he is now dead. Have you met with the letter of a Turkish cadi at the end of Layard's "Ancient Babylon"?[12] that also is refreshing, and a capital comment on the whole book which precedes it,—the Oriental genius speaking through him.

Those Brahmins "put it through."[13] They come off, or rather stand still, conquerors, with some withered arms or legs at least to show; and they are said to have cultivated the faculty of abstraction to a degree unknown to Europeans.[14] If we cannot sing of faith and triumph, we will sing our despair. We will be that kind of bird. There are day owls, and there are night owls, and each is beautiful and even musical while about its business.

Might you not find some positive work to do with your back to Church and State, letting your back do all the rejection of them? Can you not *go* upon your pilgrimage, Peter,[15] along the winding mountain path whither you face? A step more will make those funereal church bells over your shoulder sound far and sweet as a natural sound.

"Work,—work,—work!"

Why not make a *very large* mud-pie and bake it in the sun! Only put no Church nor State into it, nor upset any other pepper box that way. Dig out a woodchuck,—for that has nothing to do with rotting institutions. Go ahead.[16]

Whether a man spends his day in an ecstasy or despondency, he must do some work to show for it, even as there are flesh and bones to show for him. We are superior to the joy we experience.

Your last two letters, methinks, have more nerve and will in them than usual, as if you had erected yourself more. Why are not they good work, if you only had a hundred correspondents to tax you?

Make your failure tragical by the earnestness and steadfastness of your endeavor, and then it will not differ from success.

Prove it to be the inevitable fate of mortals,—of one mortal,— if you can.

You said that you were writing on Immortality. I wish you would communicate to me what you know about that. You are sure to live while that is your theme.

Thus I write on some text which a sentence of your letters may have furnished.

I think of coming to see you as soon as I get a new coat, if I have money enough left. I will write to you again about it.

≈ *Letter Fifteen*

January 21, 1854, Saturday; Concord, Massachusetts

Thoreau left for Worcester at noon on January 23 and
returned to Concord at noon on January 25. From 9 a.m. to 4 p.m. on
January 24, which Thoreau noted in his journal was "a very cold day," he
and Blake walked the six miles or so from Blake's house near downtown
Worcester north to the small town of Holden and back. Thoreau was at
this date almost done with his *Walden* manuscript, which he would soon
present to the Boston publishers Ticknor and Fields.

Concord Jan 21st '54

Mr Blake,

My coat is at last done, and my mother & sister allow that I
am *so far* in a condition to go abroad. I feel as if I had gone
abroad the moment I put it on. It is, as usual a production
strange to me, the wearer, invented by some Count D'Orsay,[1]
and the maker of it was not acquainted with any of my real
depressions or elevations. He only measured a peg to hang it
on, and might have made the loop big enough to go over my
head. It requires a not quite innocent indifference not to say
insolence to wear it. Ah, the process by which we get overcoats
is not what it should be. Though the church declare it right-
eous & its priest pardons me, my own Good Genius tells me
that it is hasty & coarse & false. I expect a time when, or rather
an integrity by which a man will get his coat as honestly, and as
perfectly fitting as a tree its bark. Now our garments are typical of our conformity to the ways of the world, i.e. of the Devil,
& to some extent react on us and poison us like that shirt which
Hercules put on.[2]

I think to come & see you next week on Monday if nothing hinders. I have just returned from Court at Cambridge, whither I was called as a witness, having surveyed a water-privilege about which there is a dispute since you were here.[3]

Ah! what foreign countries there are, greater in extent than the U. S. or Russia, and with no more souls to a square mile— stretching away on every side from every human being with whom you have no sympathy. Their humanity affects me as simply monstrous. Rocks—earth—brute beasts comparatively are not so strange to me. When I sit in the parlors or kitchens of some with whom my business brings me—I was going to say in contact—(business, like misery, makes strange bedfellows)[4] I feel a sort of awe and as forlorn as if I were cast away on a des- olate shore—I think of Riley's Narrative & his sufferings.[5] You who soared like a merlin[6] with your mate through the realms of ether—in the presence of the unlike drop at once to earth a mere amorphous squab—divested of your air-inflated pinions. (By the way, excuse this writing, for I am using the stub of the last feather I chance to possess.) You travel on, however, through this dark & desert world. You see in the distance an intelligent & sympathizing lineament,—stars come forth in the dark & oases appear in the desert.

But (to return to the subject of coats), we are well nigh smothered under yet more fatal coats, which do not fit us, our whole lives long. Consider the cloak that our employment or station is—how rarely men treat each other for what in their true & naked characters they are. How we use & tolerate pre- tension; how the judge is clothed with dignity which does not belong to him, and the trembling witness with humility that does not belong to him, and the criminal perchance with shame or impudence which no more belong to him. It does not matter so much then what is the fashion of the cloak with which we cloak these cloaks. Change the coat—put the judge in the criminal box & the criminal on the bench, and you might think that you had changed the men.

No doubt the thinnest of all cloaks is conscious deception or lies, it is sleazy & frays out, it is not close woven like cloth—but its meshes are a coarse net-work. A man can afford to lie only at the intersection of the threads, but truth puts in the filling & makes a consistent stuff.

I mean merely to suggest how much the station affects the demeanor & self-respectability of the parties, & that the difference between the judge's coat of cloth & the criminal's is insignificant compared with—or only partially significant of the difference between the coats which their respective stations permits them to wear. What airs the judge may put on over his coat which the criminal may not! The judge's opinion (*sententia*) of the criminal *sentences* him & is read by the clerk of the court, & published to the world, & executed by the sheriff—but the criminal's opinion of the judge has the weight of a sentence & is published & executed only in the supreme court of the universe—a court not of common pleas.[7] How much juster is the one than the other? Men are continually *sentencing* each other, but whether we be judges or criminals, the sentence is ineffectual unless we condemn ourselves.

I am glad to hear that I do not always limit your vision when you look this way—that you sometimes see the light through me, that I am here & there windows & not all dead wall. Might not the community sometimes petition a man to remove himself as a nuisance—a darkener of the day—a too large mote?

H. D. T.

⁂ Letter Sixteen

August 8, 1854, Tuesday; Concord, Massachusetts

Thoreau wrote this letter the day before *Walden* was published. In late May, at about the time he had completed his work on the proofs of his new book, Anthony Burns was arrested in Boston under the provisions of the Fugitive Slave Law. With about 50,000 citizens lining the streets, Burns was escorted by federal troops from the Boston courthouse to a federal frigate, which remanded him to his owner in Virginia. A month later, on Independence Day, Thoreau read an extract from his essay "Slavery in Massachusetts" at an antislavery gathering in Framingham, Massachusetts. The full essay was given wide exposure by being reprinted in *The Liberator* on July 21 and on August 2 in the *New-York Tribune*. At the same gathering and on the same stage, the fiery abolitionist William Lloyd Garrison (1805–1879) burned a copy of the U.S. Constitution, declaring it "a covenant with death and an agreement with hell" because of its provisions allowing slavery to stand. As he mentions at the beginning of the next letter, the day after he wrote this letter he took the train into Boston to pick up his author's copies of *Walden* from the publisher, Ticknor and Fields, and had the publisher send a copy of the book to Blake.

Concord, August 8, 1854.

Mr. Blake,—

Methinks I have spent a rather unprofitable summer thus far. I have been too much with the world, as the poet might say.[1] The completest performance of the highest duties it imposes would yield me but little satisfaction. Better the neglect of all such, because your life passed on a level where it was impossible to recognize them. Latterly, I have heard the very flies buzz too distinctly, and have accused myself because I did not still this superficial din. We must not be too easily distracted by the crying of children or of dynasties. The Irishman erects his sty, and gets drunk, and jabbers more and more under my eaves, and I am responsible for all that filth and folly. I find it, as ever, very unprofitable to have much to do with men. It is sowing the wind, but not reaping even the whirlwind;[2] only reaping an unprofitable calm and stagnation. Our conversation is a smooth, and civil, and never-ending speculation merely. I take up the thread of it again in the morning, with very much such courage as the invalid takes his prescribed Seidlitz powders.[3] Shall I help you to some of the mackerel?[4] It would be more respectable if men, as has been said before, instead of being such pigmy desperates, were Giant Despairs.[5] Emerson[6] says that his life is so unprofitable and shabby for the most part, that he is driven to all sorts of resources, and, among the rest, to men. I tell him that we differ only in our resources. Mine is to get away from men. They very rarely affect me as grand or beautiful; but I know that there is a sunrise and a sunset every day. In the summer, this world is a mere watering-place,—a Saratoga,—drinking so many tumblers of Congress water;[7] and in the winter, is it any better, with its oratorios? I have seen more men than usual, lately; and, well as I was acquainted with one, I am surprised to find what vulgar fellows they are. They do a little business commonly each day, in order to pay their board, and then they congregate in sitting-rooms and feebly fabulate and paddle in the social slush; and when I think that they have sufficiently relaxed, and am prepared to see them steal away to their shrines, they go unashamed to their beds, and take on a new layer of sloth. They may be single, or have families in their *faineancy*.[8] I do not meet men who can have nothing to do with me because they have so much to do with themselves. However, I trust that a very few cherish purposes which they never declare. Only think, for a moment, of a man about his affairs! How we should respect him! How glorious he would appear! Not working for any corporation, its agent, or president, but fulfilling the end of his being! A man about *his business* would be the cynosure of all eyes.[9]

The other evening I was determined that I would silence this shallow din; that I would walk in various directions and see if there was not to be found any depth of silence around. As Bonaparte sent out his horsemen in the Red Sea on all sides to find shallow water,[10] so I sent forth my mounted thoughts to find deep water. I left the village and paddled up the river to Fair Haven Pond.[11] As the sun went down, I saw a solitary boatman disporting on the smooth lake. The falling dews seemed to strain and purify the air, and I was soothed with an infinite stillness. I got the world, as it were, by the nape of the neck, and held it under in the tide of its own events, till it was drowned, and then I let it go down stream like a dead dog. Vast hollow chambers of silence stretched away on every side, and my being expanded in proportion, and filled them. Then first could I appreciate sound, and find it musical.

But now for your news. Tell us of the year. Have you fought the good fight?[12] What is the state of your crops? Will your harvest answer well to the seed-time, and are you cheered by the prospect of stretching corn-fields? Is there any blight on your fields, any murrain in your herds? Have you tried the size and quality of your potatoes? It does one good to see their balls dangling in the lowlands. Have you got your meadow hay before the fall rains shall have set in? Is there enough in your barns to keep your cattle over? Are you killing weeds nowadays? or have you earned leisure to go a-fishing? Did you plant any Giant Regrets last spring, such as I saw advertised?[13] It is not a new species, but the result of cultivation and a fertile soil. They are excellent for sauce. How is it with your marrow squashes for winter use? Is there likely to be a sufficiency of fall feed in your neighborhood? What is the state of the springs? I read that in your country there is more water on the hills than in the valleys.[14] Do you find it easy to get all the help you require? Work early and late, and let your men and teams rest at noon. Be careful not to drink too much sweetened water,[15] while at your hoeing, this hot weather. You can bear the heat much better for it.

༄ Letter Seventeen

September 21, 1854, Thursday; Concord, Massachusetts

By this date at least sixty-two reviews of *Walden* had appeared, mostly in newspapers, as was most common for the time, and most of the reviews were highly laudatory. Thinking that he could capitalize on the apparent success of his new book, Thoreau began planning a lecture tour to the West. At this time, however, he only had his long "Walking" lecture to work with, so he split that into four sections and began working each into a separate lecture. The "introductory" lecture to the course he titled "Moonlight"; the other three lectures he titled "Walking" and "The Wild," which required very little work, and "What Shall It Profit," which required a great deal of work and was not actually completed until late November or early December.

Concord, September 21, 1854.

Blake,—

I have just read your letter, but do not mean now to answer it, solely for want of time to say what I wish. I directed a copy of "Walden" to you at Ticknor's, on the day of its publication, and it should have reached you before. I am encouraged to know that it interests you as it now stands,—a printed book,— for you apply a very severe test to it,—you make the highest demand on me. As for the excursion you speak of,[1] I should like it right well,—indeed I thought of proposing the same thing to you and Brown, some months ago. Perhaps it would have been better if I had done so then; for in that case I should have been able to enter into it with that infinite margin to my views,—spotless of all engagements,—which I think so necessary. As it is, I have agreed to go a-lecturing to Plymouth,[2] Sunday after next (October 1), and to Philadelphia[3] in November, and thereafter to the West, *if they shall want me;* and, as I have pre-pared nothing in that shape, I feel as if my hours were spoken for. However, I think that, after having been to Plymouth, I may take a day or two—if that date will suit you and Brown. *At any rate* I will write you then.

☙ *Letter Eighteen*

October 5, 1854, Thursday; Concord, Massachusetts

Thomas Cholmondeley (b. 1823?) had arrived in Concord with letters of introduction to Emerson, who suggested he board at the Thoreau family home. According to Thoreau's biographer, Walter Harding, "Cholmondeley immediately took to Thoreau and lost all interest in Emerson." When Cholmondeley finally left for England, he asked Thoreau to accompany him, but according to Harding, Thoreau responded that "he was too attached to his native Concord to think of going abroad."

Concord Oct. 5 '54

Mr. Blake,

After I wrote to you Mr. Watson postponed my going to Plymouth one week i.e. till next Sunday, and now he wishes me to carry my instruments & survey his grounds, to which he has been adding. Since I want a little money, though I contemplate but a short excursion, I do not feel at liberty to decline this work. I do not know exactly how long it will detain me—but there is plenty of time yet—& I will write to you again—perhaps from Plymouth—

There is a Mr. Thomas Cholmondeley (pronounced Chumly), a young English author, staying at our house at present—who asks me to teach him *botany*—i.e. anything which I know—and also to make an excursion to some mountain with him. He is a well-behaved person, and *possibly* I may propose his taking that run to Wachusett with us—if it will be agreeable to

you. Nay. If I do not hear any objection from you I will consider myself *at liberty* to invite him.

                                    In haste,
                                    H. D. Thoreau

❧ Letter Nineteen

October 14, 1854, Saturday; Concord, Massachusetts

Thoreau delivered his new "Moonlight" lecture at Leyden Hall in Plymouth, Massachusetts, on Sunday evening, October 7. Accompanied by both Blake and Cholmondeley, he ascended Mount Wachusett on Thursday, October 19. Westminster and Princeton Center are the nearest towns north and south of Mount Wachusett, respectively.

Concord Sat. pm. Oct 14 '54

Blake,

I have just returned from Plymouth, where I have been detained surveying much longer than I expected.

What do you say to visiting Wachusett next Thursday? I will start at 7¼ a.m. *unless there is a prospect of a stormy day*, go by cars to Westminster, & thence on foot 5 or 6 miles to the *mt* tops, where I may engage to meet you at (or before) 12. *m.*

If the weather is unfavorable, I will try again—on Friday,—& again on Monday.

If a storm comes on after starting, I will seek you at the tavern in Princeton Center, as soon as circumstances will permit.

I shall expect an answer to clinch the bargain.

Yrs

Henry D. Thoreau.

ᴚ Letter Twenty

December 19, 1854, Tuesday; Concord, Massachusetts

Because he had not received enough invitations to make it worth his while, Thoreau was forced to give up his plans for a lecture tour to the West and instead began accepting engagements nearer to home. He had delivered his new "What Shall It Profit" lecture in Railroad Hall in Providence, Rhode Island, on December 6, meeting Theo Brown while in town and thereby setting up the pun which begins this letter.

Concord, December 19, 1854.

Mr. Blake,—

I suppose you have heard of my truly providential meeting with Mr T. Brown; providential because it saved me from the suspicion that my words had fallen altogether on stony ground, when it turned out that there was some Worcester soil there. You will allow me to consider that I correspond with him through you.

I confess that I am a very bad correspondent, so far as promptness of reply is concerned; but then I am sure to answer sooner or later. The longer I have forgotten you, the more I remember you. For the most part I have not been idle since I saw you. How does the world go with you? or rather, how do you get along without it? I have not yet learned to live, that I can see, and I fear that I shall not very soon. I find, however, that in the long run things correspond to my original idea,— that they correspond to nothing else so much; and thus a man may really be a true prophet without any great exertion. The day is never so dark, nor the night even, but that the laws at least of light still prevail, and so may make it light in our minds if they are open to the truth. There is considerable danger that a man will be crazy between dinner and supper; but it will not directly answer any good purpose that I know of, and it is just as easy to be sane. We have got to know what both life and death are, before we can begin to live after our own fashion. Let us be learning our a-b-c's as soon as possible. I never yet knew the sun to be knocked down and rolled through a mud-puddle; he comes out honor-bright from behind every storm. Let us then take sides with the sun, seeing we have so much leisure. Let us not put all we prize into a football to be kicked, when a bladder will do as well.

When an Indian is burned,[1] his body may be broiled, it may be no more than a beefsteak. What of that? They may broil his *heart*, but they do not therefore broil his *courage*,—his principles. Be of good courage![2] That is the main thing.

If a man were to place himself in an attitude to bear manfully the greatest evil that can be inflicted on him, he would find suddenly that there was no such evil to bear; his brave back would go a-begging. When Atlas got his back made up,[3] that was all that was required. (In this case α *priv.*, not *pleon.*, and τλῆμ.)[4] The world rests on principles. The wise gods will never make underpinning of a man. But as long as he crouches, and skulks, and shirks his work, every creature that has weight will be treading on his toes, and crushing him; he will himself tread with one foot on the other foot.

The monster is never just there where we think he is. What is truly monstrous is our cowardice and sloth.

Have no idle disciplines like the Catholic Church[5] and others; have only positive and fruitful ones. Do what you know you ought to do. Why should we ever go abroad, even across the way, to ask a neighbor's advice? There is a nearer neighbor within us incessantly telling us how we should behave.[6] But we wait for the neighbor without to tell us of some false, easier way.

They have a census-table[7] in which they put down the number of the insane. Do you believe that they put them all down there? Why, in every one of these houses there is at least one man fighting or squabbling a good part of his time with a dozen pet demons of his own breeding and cherishing, which are relentlessly gnawing at his vitals; and if perchance he resolve at length that he will courageously combat them, he says, "Ay! ay! I will attend to you after dinner!" And, when that time comes, he concludes that he is good for another stage, and reads a column or two about the *Eastern War!*[8] Pray, to be in earnest, where is Sevastopol? Who is Menchikoff? and Nicholas behind there? who the Allies? Did not we fight a little (little enough to be sure, but just enough to make it interesting) at Alma, at Balaclava, at Inkermann? We love to fight far from home. Ah! the Minié musket is the king of weapons. Well, let us get one then.

I just put another stick into my stove,—a pretty large mass of white oak. How many men will do enough this cold winter to pay for the fuel that will be required to warm them? I suppose I have burned up a pretty good-sized tree to-night,—and for what? I settled with Mr. Tarbell[9] for it the other day; but that wasn't the final settlement. I got off cheaply from him. At last, one will say, "Let us see, how much wood did you burn, sir?" And I shall shudder to think that the next question will be, "What did you do while you were warm?" Do we think the ashes will pay for it? that God is an ash-man? It is a fact that we have got to render an account for the deeds done in the body.[10]

Who knows but we shall be better the next year than we have been the past? At any rate, I wish you a really *new* year,—commencing from the instant you read this,—and happy or unhappy, according to your deserts.

ᗠ *Letter Twenty-one*

December 22, 1854, Friday; Concord, Massachusetts

At all three of the lectures Thoreau mentions in this letter—in the seaport city of New Bedford, on the island of Nantucket
south of Cape Cod, and in Worcester—he delivered "What Shall It
Profit," the essay version of which was posthumously published as "Life
without Principle." Daniel Ricketson (1813–1898), his host in New
Bedford, was an eccentric, independently wealthy Quaker, sometime historian, and nature lover whom Thoreau describes well in Letter 25.
Ricketson had read *Walden* immediately upon its publication and had
written Thoreau an admiring letter on August 12. Although most scholars believe that the highly flattering review of *Walden* which appeared in
the *National Anti-Slavery Standard* on December 16, 1854, was written by
novelist, editor, journalist, scholar, and ardent antislavery activist Lydia
Maria Child (1802–1880), a few sentences in the review suggest Blake
may have been the author. One such sentence reads: "It is refreshing to
find . . . the sentiments of one man whose aim manifestly is to *live*, and
not to waste his time upon the externals of living." The abbreviation
"inst." (for "instant") in the second paragraph means "during the present or current month."

Concord Dec. 22nd '54

Mr Blake,

I will lecture for your Lyceum on the 4th of January next;
and I hope that I shall have time for that good day out of doors.
Mr Cholmondeley is in Boston, yet *perhaps* I may write him to
accompany me.

I have engaged to lecture at New Bedford on the 26 inst.,
stopping with Daniel Ricketson 3 miles out of town; and at
Nantucket on the 28th; so that I shall be gone all next week.

They say there is some danger of being weather-bound at Nantucket, but I see that others run the same risk.

You had better acknowledge the receipt of this at any rate, though you should write nothing else, otherwise I shall not know whether you get it; but perhaps you will not wait till you have seen me to answer my letter. I will tell you what I think of lecturing when I see you.

Did you see the notice of Walden in the last Anti-Slavery Standard? You will not be surprised if I tell you that it reminded me of you.

Yrs,

Henry D. Thoreau.

ᝠ Letter Twenty-two

June 27, 1855, Wednesday; Concord, Massachusetts

The weakness in his legs that Thoreau suffered throughout the remainder of this year and into the next was very likely a symptom of tuberculosis. Given his known susceptibility to psychosomatic illness (he suffered acutely from sympathetic lockjaw in the weeks after his older brother John died of the disease), one suspects that the weakness may have been brought about by *Walden* not being as well received as he had hoped. In any case, the debility caused him to postpone what would have been his third trip to Maine; instead he went on what amounted to a convalescent excursion to Cape Cod with Channing shortly after writing this letter. Neither Blake nor Brown was able to join him during his two-week stay on the Cape. Essay versions of his earlier lecture course, "An Excursion to Cape Cod," began appearing serially in *Putnam's Monthly* for June but halted peremptorily after the August issue, ostensibly because Curtis, still the editor, had not realized that "the Cape Cod paper 'was to be expanded into a book,' " by which he apparently meant that the whole was longer than he was willing to accommodate.

Concord June 27th 1855

Mr Blake,

I have been sick and good for nothing but to lie on my back and wait for something to turn up, for two or three months. This has *compelled* me to postpone several things, among them writing to you to whom I am so deeply in debt, and inviting you and Brown to Concord—not having brains adequate to such an exertion. I should feel a little less ashamed if I could give any name to my disorder, but I cannot, and our doctor cannot help me to it, and I will not take the name of any disease in vain.[1] However, there is one consolation in being sick, and that is the possibility that you may recover to a better state than you were ever in before. I expected in the winter to be deep in the woods of Maine in my canoe long before this, but I am so far from that that I can only take a languid walk in Concord streets.

I do not know how the mistake arose about the Cape Cod excursion. The nearest I have come to that with anybody is that about a month ago Channing proposed to me to go to Truro, on Cape Cod, with him & board there awhile, but I declined. For a week past however I have been a little inclined to go there & sit on the sea-shore a week or more, but I do not venture to propose myself as the companion of him or of any peripatetic man. Not that I should not rejoice to have you and Brown or C. sitting there also. I am not sure that C. really wishes to go now—and as I go simply for the medicine of it, while I need it, I should not think it worth the while to notify him when I am about to take my bitters.[2]

Since I began this, or within 5 minutes, I have begun to think that I will start for Truro next Saturday morning—the 30th. I do not know at what hour the packet[3] leaves Boston, nor exactly what kind of accommodation I shall find at Truro.

I should be singularly favored if you and Brown were there at the same time, and though you speak of the 20th of July, I will be so bold as to suggest your coming to Concord Friday night (when, by the way, Garrison & Phillips[4] hold forth here) & going to the Cape with me. Though we take short walks together there we can have *long* talks, and you & Brown will have time enough for your own excursions besides.

I received a letter from Cholmondeley last winter,[5] which I should like to show you, as well as his book. He said that he had "accepted the offer of a captaincy in the Salop Militia," and was hoping to take an active part in the war before long.

I thank you again and again for the encouragement your letters are to me. But I must stop this writing, or I shall have to pay for it.

Yours Truly

H. D. Thoreau

≫ Letter Twenty-three

July 8, 1855, Sunday; North Truro, Massachusetts

The Highland Lighthouse is on the Atlantic side of the Cape
in the town of North Truro at about the same latitude as the southern-
most part of Provincetown ($42.0405°N$), which is on the southern or
bayside shore of the northern extremity of the Cape. Commerce Street
seems to be an error for Commercial Street; Boston maps of the time
show no Commerce Street but a Commercial Street paralleling the harbor from the foot of Long Wharf on the eastern side of the Boston
peninsula around the northern tip of the peninsula to the Charles River
(now Charlestown) Bridge. T Wharf was an extension jutting northward
from about the center of Long Wharf and then running parallel to Long
Wharf in an easterly direction. Long Wharf was and still is an extension
into the harbor of State Street. As one might expect, "good livers" are
those who know how to enjoy the pleasures of life.

North Truro, July 8, 1855.

There being no packet, I did not leave Boston till last Thursday, though I came down on Wednesday, and Channing with
me. There is no public house here; but we are boarding with Mr.
James Small, the keeper, in a little house attached to the Highland Lighthouse. It is true the table is not so clean as could be
desired, but I have found it much superior in that respect to the
Provincetown hotel. They are what is called "good livers." Our
host has another larger and very good house, within a quarter
of a mile, unoccupied, where he says he can accommodate several more. He is a very good man to deal with,—has often been
the representative of the town, and is perhaps the most intelligent man in it. I shall probably stay here as much as ten days

longer: board $3.50 per week. So you and Brown had better come down forthwith. You will find either the schooner Melrose or another, or both, leaving Commerce Street, or else T Wharf, at 9 A. M. (it commonly means 10), Tuesdays, Thursdays, and Saturdays,—if not other days. We left about 10 A. M., and reached Provincetown at 5 P. M.,—a very good run. A stage runs up the Cape every morning but Sunday, starting at 4½ A. M., and reaches the post office in North Truro, seven miles from Provincetown, and one from the lighthouse, about 6 o'clock. If you arrive at P. before night, you can walk over, and leave your baggage to be sent. You can also come by cars from Boston to Yarmouth, and thence by stage forty miles more,— through every day, but it costs much more, and is not so pleasant. Come by all means, for it is the best place to see the ocean in these States. I *hope* I shall be worth meeting.

🪶 *Letter Twenty-four*

July 14, 1855, Saturday; North Truro, Massachusetts

Thoreau and Channing did indeed return to Concord from the Cape on Wednesday, July 18. To go *"before the mast"* means to serve as a common sailor and therefore be quartered in the forward part of a ship, as opposed to the officers, mates, and passengers, whose quarters were *behind* the mast. Richard Henry Dana (1815–1882), who graduated from Harvard College the same year as Thoreau (1837), had published his well-known travel book *Two Years before the Mast* in 1840.

July 14.

You say that you hope I will excuse your frequent writing. I trust you will excuse my infrequent and curt writing until I am able to resume my old habits, which for three months I have been compelled to abandon. Methinks I am beginning to be better. I think to leave the Cape next Wednesday, and so shall not see you here; but I shall be glad to meet you in Concord, though I may not be able to go *before the mast,* in a boating excursion. This is an admirable place for coolness and sea-bathing and retirement. You must come prepared for cool weather and fogs.

P.S.—There is no mail up till Monday morning.

☙ Letter Twenty-five

September 26, 1855, Wednesday; Concord, Massachusetts

The weakness Thoreau continued to experience in his legs portended ill for his artistry because, as he often suggested in his journal, his literary output was in fairly direct proportion to his peripatetic exertions. He appears not to have felt quite himself again until the spring.

Concord, September 26, 1855.

Mr. Blake,—

The other day I thought that my health must be better,—that I gave at last a sign of vitality,—because I experienced a slight chagrin. But I do not see how strength is to be got into my legs again. These months of feebleness have yielded few, if any, thoughts, though they have not passed without serenity, such as our sluggish Musketaquid[1] suggests. I hope that the harvest is to come. I trust that you have at least warped up the stream a little daily, holding fast by your anchors at night, since I saw you, and have kept my place for me while I have been absent.

Mr. Ricketson of New Bedford has just made me a visit of a day and a half, and I have had a quite good time with him. He and Channing have got on particularly well together. He is a man of very simple tastes, notwithstanding his wealth; a lover of nature; but, above all, singularly frank and plain-spoken. I think that you might enjoy meeting him.

Sincerity is a great but rare virtue, and we pardon to it much complaining, and the betrayal of many weaknesses. R. says of himself, that he sometimes thinks that he has all the infirmities of genius without the genius; is wretched without a hair-pillow, etc.; expresses a great and awful uncertainty with regard to "God," "Death," his "immortality"; says, "If I only knew," etc. He loves Cowper's "Task" better than anything else; and thereafter, perhaps, Thomson, Gray, and even Howitt.[2] He has evidently suffered for want of sympathizing companions. He says that he sympathizes with much in my books, but much in them is naught to him,—"namby-pamby,"—"stuff,"—"mystical." Why will not I, having common sense, write in plain English always; *teach* men in detail how to live a simpler life, etc.; not go off into ———? But I say that I have no scheme about it,—no designs on men at all; and, if I had, my mode would be to tempt them with the fruit, and not with the manure. To what end do I lead a simple life at all, pray? That I may teach others to simplify their lives?—and so all our lives be *simplified* merely, like an algebraic formula? Or not, rather, that I may make use of the ground I have cleared, to live more worthily and profitably? I would fain lay the most stress forever on that which is the most important,—imports the most to me,—though it were only (what it is likely to be) a vibration in the air. As a preacher, I should be prompted to tell men, not so much how to get their wheat-bread cheaper, as of the bread of life[3] compared with which *that* is bran. Let a man only taste these loaves, and he becomes a skillful economist at once. He'll not waste much time in earning those. Don't spend your time in drilling soldiers, who may turn out hirelings after all, but give to undrilled peasantry a *country* to fight for.[4] The schools begin with what they call the elements,[5] and where do they end?

I was glad to hear the other day that Higginson and Brown were gone to Ktaadn[6]; it must be so much better to go to than a Woman's Rights or Abolition Convention; better still, to the delectable primitive mounts[7] within you, which you have dreamed of from your youth up, and seen, perhaps, in the horizon, but never climbed.

But how do *you* do? Is the air sweet to you? Do you find anything at which you can work, accomplishing something solid from day to day? Have you put sloth and doubt behind, considerably?—had one redeeming dream this summer? I dreamed, last night, that I could vault over any height it pleased me. That was *something*; and I contemplated myself with a slight satisfaction in the morning for it.

Methinks I will write to you. Methinks you will be glad to hear. We will stand on solid foundations to one another,—I a column planted on this shore, you on that. We meet the same sun in his rising. We were built slowly, and have come to our bearing. We will not mutually fall over that we may meet, but will grandly and eternally guard the straits. Methinks I see an inscription on you, which the architect made, the stucco being worn off to it. The name of that ambitious worldly king is crumbling away.[8] I see it toward sunset in favorable lights. Each must read for the other, as might a sailer-by. Be sure you are star-y-pointing[9] still. How is it on your side? I will not require an answer until you think I have paid my debts to you.

I have just got a letter from Ricketson, urging me to come to New Bedford, which possibly I may do. He says I can wear my old clothes there.

Let me be remembered in your quiet house.

﹡ Letter Twenty-six

December 9, 1855, Sunday; Concord, Massachusetts

Thoreau took Blake in his boat up the Assabet River in Concord on November 9, both to collect wood for the coming winter (a highly significant annual ritual for Thoreau, one discussed in the "Housewarming" chapter of *Walden* as well as in this letter) and to salvage from the river planks and driftwood with which to build a suitable bookshelf for the books Cholmondeley had sent from England (see note 12 to this letter). As Thoreau remarks, the books arrived on November 30—appropriately enough, aboard a ship named *Asia*.

Concord, December 9, 1855.

Mr. Blake,—

Thank you! thank you for going a-wooding with me,—and enjoying it,—for being warmed by my wood fire. I have indeed enjoyed it much alone. I see how I might enjoy it yet more with company,—how we might help each other to live. And to be admitted to Nature's hearth costs nothing. None is excluded, but excludes himself. You have only to push aside the curtain.[1]

I am glad to hear that you were there too. There are many more such voyages, and longer ones, to be made on that river, for it is the water of life. The Ganges[2] is nothing to it. Observe its reflections,—no idea but is familiar to it. That river, though to dull eyes it seems terrestrial wholly, flows through Elysium.[3] What powers bathe in it invisible to villagers! Talk of its shallowness,—that hay-carts can be driven through it at midsummer; its depth passeth my understanding.[4] If, forgetting the allurements of the world, I could drink deeply[5] enough of it; if, cast adrift from the shore, I could with complete integrity float on it, I should never be seen on the Mill-dam[6] again. If there is any depth in me, there is a corresponding depth in it. It is the cold blood of the gods. I paddle and bathe in their artery.

I do not want a stick of wood for so trivial a use as to burn even, but they get it over night, and carve and gild it that it may please my eye. What persevering lovers they are! What infinite pains to attract and delight us! They will supply us with fagots wrapped in the daintiest packages, and freight paid; sweet-scented woods, and bursting into flower, and resounding as if Orpheus[7] had just left them,—these shall be our fuel, and we still prefer to chaffer with the wood-merchant!

The jug we found[8] still stands draining bottom up on the bank, on the sunny side of the house. That river,—who shall say exactly whence it came, and whither it goes? Does aught that flows come from a higher source? Many things drift downward on its surface which would enrich a man. If you could only be on the alert all day, and every day! And the nights are as long as the days.[9]

Do you not think you could contrive thus to get woody fibre enough to bake your wheaten bread with? Would you not perchance have tasted the sweet crust of another kind of bread in the mean while, which ever hangs ready baked on the bread-fruit trees of the world?

Talk of burning your smoke after the wood has been consumed![10] There is a far more important and warming heat, commonly lost, which precedes the burning of the wood. It is the smoke of industry, which is incense. I had been so thoroughly warmed in body and spirit, that when at length my fuel was housed, I came near selling it to the ash-man, as if I had extracted all its heat.

You should have been here to help me get in my boat. The last time I used it, November 27th, paddling up the Assabet, I saw a great round pine log sunk deep in the water, and with labor got it aboard. When I was floating this home so gently, it occurred to me why I had found it. It was to make wheels with to roll my boat into winter quarters upon. So I sawed off two thick rollers from one end, pierced them for wheels, and then of a joist which I had found drifting on the river in the summer I made an axletree, and on this I rolled my boat out.

Miss Mary Emerson[11] is here,—the youngest person in Concord, though about eighty,—and the most apprehensive of a genuine thought; earnest to know of your inner life; most stimulating society; and exceedingly witty withal. She says they called her old when she was young, and she has never grown any older. I wish you could see her.

My books[12] did not arrive till November 30th, the cargo of the Asia having been complete when they reached Liverpool. I have arranged them in a case which I made in the mean while, partly of river boards. I have not dipped far into the new ones yet. One is splendidly bound and illuminated. They are in English, French, Latin, Greek, and Sanscrit. I have not made out the significance of this godsend yet.

Farewell, and bright dreams to you!

≈ *Letter Twenty-seven*

March 13, 1856, Thursday; Concord, Massachusetts

Thoreau's exploration in this letter of the spring sugaring season's metaphorical implications shows his frame of mind as he went out the following day, March 14, to see if he could find sap flowing in maple trees. After using his knife to tap several white maples, none of which flowed, he discovered a red maple whose "limb was moistened by sap trickling along the bark. Tapping this, I was surprised to find it flow freely." He spent the entire week tapping maples, collecting sap, and boiling the sap down for sugar. At the end of the week he got into a dispute with his father, who pointed out that the time-consuming process kept Thoreau from his studies. "I made it my study," Thoreau replied. "I felt as if I had been to a university."

Concord Mar. 13 1856.

Mr Blake—

It is high time I sent you a word. I have not heard from Harrisburg since offering to go there,[1] and have not been invited to lecture anywhere else the past winter. So you see I am fast growing rich. This is quite right, for such is my relation to the lecture-goers. I should be surprised and alarmed if there were any great call for me. I confess that I am considerably alarmed even when I hear that an individual wishes to meet me, for my experience teaches me that we shall thus only be made certain of a mutual strangeness, which otherwise we might never have been aware of.

I have not yet recovered strength enough for such a walk as you propose,[2] though pretty well again for circumscribed rambles & chamber work. Even now I am probably the greatest walker in Concord—to its disgrace be it said. I remember our walks & talks & sailing in the past, with great satisfaction, and trust that we shall have more of them ere long—have more woodings-up—for even in the spring we must still seek "fuel to maintain our fires."[3]

As you suggest, we would fain value one another for what we are absolutely, rather than relatively. How will this do for a symbol of sympathy?[4]

As for compliments,—even the stars praise me, and I praise them,—they & I sometimes belong to a mutual admiration society. Is it not so with you? I know you of old. Are you not tough & earnest to be talked at, praised or blamed? Must *you* go out of the room because you are the subject of conversation? Where will you go to—pray? Shall we look into the "Letter Writer"[5] to see what compliments are admissible. I am not afraid of praise for I have practised it on myself. As for my deserts, I never took an account of that stock, and in this connection care not whether I am deserving or not. When I hear praise coming do I not elevate & arch myself to hear it like the sky, and as impersonally? Think I appropriate any of it to my weak legs? No—praise away *till all is blue.*[6]

I see by the newspapers[7] that the season for making sugar is at hand. Now is the time, whether you be rock or white maple,—or hickory. I trust that you have prepared a store of sap tubs and sumach spouts, and invested largely in kettles.

Early the first frosty morning tap your maples—the sap will not run in summer, you know— It matters not how little juice you get, if you get all you can, and boil it down. I made just one crystal of sugar once, one twentieth of an inch cube out of a pumpkin, & it sufficed. Though the yield be no greater than that,—this is not less the reason for it, & it will be not the less sweet,—nay, it will be infinitely the sweeter.

Shall then the maple yield sugar, & not man? Shall the farmer be thus active, & surely have so much sugar to show for it before this very March is gone,—while I read the newspaper? While he works in his sugar camp, let me work in mine—for sweetness is in me, & to sugar it shall come;—it shall not all go to leaves & wood. Am I not a *sugar maple* man then?

Boil down the sweet sap which the spring causes to flow within you— Stop not at syrup; go on to sugar,—though you present the world with but a single crystal—a crystal not made from trees in your yard, but from the new life that stirs in your pores. Cheerfully skim your kettle, & watch it set & crystal-ize—making a holiday of it, if you will. Heaven will be propitious to you as to him.

Say to the farmer,—There is your crop,—Here is mine. Mine is sugar to sweeten sugar with. If you will listen to me, I will sweeten your whole load,—your whole life.

Then will the callers ask—Where is Blake?—He is in his sugar-camp on the *Mt.* side.— Let the world await him.

Then will the little boys bless you, & the great boys too,—for such sugar is the origin of many condiments—Blakeians, in the shops of Worcester, of new form, with their mottos wrapped up in them.[8]

Shall men taste only the sweetness of the maple & the cane, the coming year?

A walk over the crust to Asnybumskit,[9] standing there in its inviting simplicity,—is tempting to think of,—making a fire on the snow under some rock! The very poverty of outward nature implies an inward wealth in the walker. What a Golconda[10] is he conversant with, thawing his fingers over such a blaze! —But—but—

Have you read the new poem—"The Angel in the House"?[11]—perhaps you will find it good for you.

H. D. T.

≈ Letter Twenty-eight

May 21, 1856, Wednesday; Concord, Massachusetts

The day after Thoreau wrote this letter, Congressman Preston Brooks of South Carolina used a walking cane to beat Senator Charles Sumner of Massachusetts into unconsciousness on the floor of the Senate chambers. Sumner had delivered a strident speech on "Bleeding Kansas," where pro- and antislavery forces were violently contending with one another, and Brooks felt that Sumner had impugned the integrity of a relative. It took Sumner over three years to recover from his injuries. Thoreau does not mention this event in his journal, where he continued to concentrate heavily on observations of nature, although surely the event was a topic of conversation with Blake and Brown when they visited Concord on May 25. On the way to Fair Haven Pond, an expansion of the Sudbury River, the trio stopped at Clamshell Hill, where Thoreau found five Indian arrowheads. He had a special knack for finding arrowheads and other stone implements, in part because he knew where to look, having now studied Indian history for so many years. Thoreau reciprocated his friends' visit with an extended stay in Worcester the following month, June 13–19, rooming first at Brown's house and then at Blake's. While in Worcester he sat for a photograph at the rooms of the daguerreotypist Benjamin Maxham.

Concord May 21st '56

Mr. Blake,

I have not for a long time been *putting such thoughts together* as I should like to read to the company you speak of. I have enough of that sort to say, or even read, but not time now to arrange it. Something I have prepared might prove for their entertainment or refreshment perchance, but I would not like to have a hat carried round for it. I have just been reading some papers to see if they would do for your company; but though I thought pretty well of them as long as I read them to myself, when I got an auditor to try them on, I felt that they would not answer. How could I let you drum up a company to hear them?— In fine, what I have is either too scattered or loosely arranged, or too light, or else is too scientific and matter of fact (I run a good deal into that of late) for so hungry a company.

I am still a learner, not a teacher, feeding somewhat omnivorously, browsing both stalk & leaves—but I shall perhaps be enabled to speak with the more precision & authority by & by—if philosophy & sentiment are not buried under a multitude of details.

I do not refuse, but accept your invitation—only changing the time— I consider myself invited to Worcester once for all—& many thanks to the inviter.

As for the Harvard excursion,[1] will you let me suggest another? Do you & Brown come to Concord on Saturday, if the weather promises well, and spend the Sunday here on the river or hills or both. So we shall save some of our money, (which is of next importance to our souls) and lose—I do not know what. You say you *talked* of coming here before, now *do* it. I do not propose this because I think that I am worth your spending time with—but because I hope that we may prove flint & steel to one another. It is at most only an hour's ride further, & you can at any rate do what you please when you get here.

Then we will see if we have any apology to offer for our existence. So come to Concord!—come to Concord!—come to Concord! or————————your suit shall be defaulted.

As for the dispute about solitude & society[2] any comparison is impertinent. It is an idling down on the plain at the base of a mountain instead of climbing steadily to its top. Of course you will be glad of all the society you can get to go up with. Will you go to glory with me?[3] is the burden of the song. I love society so much that I swallowed it all at a gulp—i.e. all that came in my way. It is not that we love to be alone, but that we love to soar, and when we do soar, the company grows thinner & thinner till there is none at all. It is either the Tribune on the plain, a sermon on the mount,[4] or a very private *ecstasy* still higher up. We are not the less to aim at the summits, though the multitude does not ascend them. Use all the society that will abet you. But perhaps I do not enter into the spirit of your talk.

H.D.T.

🙊 Letter Twenty-nine

November 19, 1856, Wednesday; Perth Amboy, New Jersey

In 1852 the wealthy Quaker abolitionist Marcus Spring (1810–1874) had purchased 268 acres a little over a mile southwest of Perth Amboy, New Jersey, on the shore of Raritan Bay near the mouth of Raritan River, as the home for a cooperative community, the Raritan Bay Union. Like other utopian communities of the time, however, it faltered, failing completely in 1860. But in 1856, having renamed the area Eagleswood, Spring decided as a fiscal stopgap to subdivide the land and sell off lots. Thoreau's friend the educator and writer Amos Bronson Alcott (1799–1888) was a friend of Spring's and during a visit to Eagleswood in October 1856 suggested that Thoreau be commissioned to survey the land and, during his visit, deliver a few lectures. On the way to Eagleswood, on October 24, Thoreau stopped off in Worcester, but because Blake had gone to a horse race in Boston, the two did not meet. Thoreau instead spent the afternoon with Brown and Higginson before continuing his journey. While at Eagleswood he lectured on "Walking," "What Shall It Profit," and "Moosehunting," the latter of which he had called "An Excursion to Moosehead Lake" in December 1853. He mentions in a letter to his sister Sophia that Blake had asked him "to stop at Worcester & lecture on my return," apparently asking specifically for a repeat of "What Shall It Profit," which he had delivered in Worcester on January 4, 1855. The three other individuals he mentions in this letter are the famous editor of the *New-York Tribune*, Horace Greeley (1811–1872), who had for many years served him as an informal literary agent; the fiery abolitionist minister and extremely popular orator the Reverend Henry Ward Beecher (1813–1887), of whom he later wrote in his journal, "If Henry Ward Beecher knows so much more about God than another, if he has made some discovery of truth in this direction, I would thank him to publish it in Silliman's Journal [a scientific publication], with as few flourishes as possible"; and most particularly the poet Walt Whitman (1819–1892), whom he met at Whitman's Brooklyn home on November 10. It must have been an electric moment, this meeting of two giants of American literature, with Alcott and Whitman's mother also being present. Whitman recollected that Thoreau said to him during their meeting, "Whitman, do you have any idea that you are rather bigger and outside the average—may perhaps have immense significance?" He also recalled Thoreau confessing, "There is much in you to which I cannot accommodate myself: the defect may be mine: but the objections are there." Although it is easy to see how Victorian-era readers of *Leaves of Grass,* published in July 1855, would have found Whitman's "sensuality" and "egotism" offensive, it is to Thoreau's credit that he was able to recognize Whitman's genius despite his objections. Years later Whitman remarked of Thoreau that he "was a surprising fellow—he is not easily grasped—is elusive: yet he is one of the native forces—stands for a fact, a movement, an upheaval: Thoreau belongs to America, to the transcendental, to the protestors.... One thing about Thoreau keeps him very near to me: I refer to his lawlessness—his dissent—his going his own absolute road let hell blaze all it chooses." As Thoreau notes, Whitman maintained a routine precisely like his own: morning study and writing followed by an afternoon walk.

Eagleswood, N. J., November 19, 1856.

Mr. Blake,—

I have been here much longer than I expected, but have deferred answering you, because I could not foresee when I shall return. I do not know yet within three or four days. This uncertainty makes it impossible for me to appoint a day to meet you, until it shall be too late to hear from you again. I think, therefore, that I must go straight home. I feel some objection to reading that "What shall it profit" lecture *again* in Worcester; but if you are quite sure that it will be worth the while (it is a grave consideration), I will even make an independent journey from Concord for that purpose. I have read three of my old lectures (that included) to the Eagleswood people, and, unexpectedly, with rare success—*i.e.,* I was aware that what I was saying was silently taken in by their ears.

You must excuse me if I write mainly a business letter now, for I am sold for the time,—am merely Thoreau the surveyor here,—and solitude is scarcely obtainable in these parts.

Alcott has been here three times, and, Saturday before last, I went with him and Greeley, by invitation of the last, to G.'s farm, thirty-six miles north of New York. The next day A. and I heard Beecher preach; and what was more, we visited Whitman the next morning (A. had already seen him), and were much interested and provoked. He is apparently the greatest democrat the world has seen. Kings and aristocracy go by the board at once, as they have long deserved to. A remarkably strong though coarse nature, of a sweet disposition, and much prized by his friends. Though peculiar and rough in his exterior, his skin (all over [?]) red, he is essentially a gentleman. I am still somewhat in a quandary about him,—feel that he is essentially strange to me, at any rate; but I am surprised by the sight of him. He is very broad, but, as I have said, not fine. He said that I misapprehended him. I am not quite sure that I do. He told us that he loved to ride up and down Broadway all day on an omnibus, sitting beside the driver, listening to the roar of the carts, and sometimes gesticulating and declaiming Homer at the top of his voice. He has long been an editor and writer for the newspapers,—was editor of the "New Orleans Crescent" once; but now has no employment but to read and write in the forenoon, and walk in the afternoon, like all the rest of the scribbling gentry.

I shall probably be in Concord next week; so you can direct to me there.

⚜ Letter Thirty

December 6 and 7, 1856, Saturday and Sunday;
Concord, Massachusetts

When Thoreau left Eagleswood, he brought some of its sta-
tionery away with him and used it to write this letter, less the letterhead
engraving, as he mentions.

Concord Dec 6 '56

Mr Blake,

What is wanting above is merely an engraving of
Eagleswood, which I have used. I trust that you got a note from
me at Eagleswood about a fortnight ago. I passed thru' Worcester on the morning of the 25th of November, and spent several
hours (from 3.30 to 6.20) in the travellers' room at the Depot,
as in a dream, it now seems. As the first Harlem train unexpectedly connected with the first from Fitchburg, I did not
spend the forenoon with you, as I had anticipated, on account
of baggage &c— If it had been a seasonable hour I should have
seen you, i.e. if you had not been gone to a horse-race. But
think of making a call at half past three in the morning!
(Would it not have implied a 3 o clock in the morning courage[1]
in both you & me?) As it were ignoring the fact that mankind
are really not at home—are not out, but so deeply in that they
cannot be seen—nearly half their hours at this season of the
year. I walked up & down the Main Street at half past 5 in the
dark, and paused long in front of Brown's store trying to distinguish its features; considering whether I might safely leave
his "Putnam"[2] in the door handle, but concluded not to risk it.

Meanwhile a watchman (?) seemed to be watching me, & I moved off. Took another turn around there, a little later, and had the very earliest offer of the Transcript[3] from an urchin behind, whom I actually could not see, it was so dark. So I withdrew, wondering if you & B. would know that I had been there. You little dream who is occupying Worcester when you are all asleep. Several things occurred there that night, which I will venture to say were not put into the Transcript. A cat caught a mouse at the depot, & gave it to her kitten to play with. So that world famous tragedy goes on by night as well as by day, & nature is *emphatically* wrong.* Also I saw a young Irishman kneel before his mother, as if in prayer, while she wiped a cinder out of his eye with her tongue; and I found that it was never too late (or early?) to learn something.— These things transpired while you and B. were, to all practical purposes, no where, & good for nothing—not even for society,—not for horse-races,—nor the taking back of a Putnam's Magazine. It is true I might have recalled you to life, but it would have been a cruel act, considering the kind of life you would have come back to.

However, I would fain write to you now by broad daylight, and report to you some of my life, such as it is, and recall you to your life, which is not always lived by you, even by day light.

Blake! Blake! Are you awake? Are you aware what an everglorious morning this is? What long expected never to be repeated opportunity is now offered to get life & knowledge?

For my part I am trying to wake up,—to wring slumber out of my pores;—for, generally, I take events as unconcernedly as

*Left on the stove too long. [Thoreau's note, written at bottom of leaf.]

a fence post,—absorb wet & cold like it, and am pleasantly tick-led with lichens slowly spreading over me. Could I not be con-tent then to be a cedar post, which lasts 25 years? Would I not rather be that than the farmer that set it? or he that preaches to that farmer?—& go to the heaven of posts at last? I think I should like that as well as any would like it. But I should not care if I sprouted into a living tree, put forth leaves & flowers, & have fruit.

I am grateful for what I am & have. My thanksgiving is per-petual. It is surprising how contented one can be with nothing definite—only a sense of* existence. Well anything for variety. I am ready to try this for the next 1000 years, & exhaust it. How sweet to think of! My extremities well charred, and my intellectual part too, so that there is no danger of worm or rot for a long while. My breath is sweet to me. O how I laugh when I think of my vague indefinite riches. No run on my bank can drain it—for my wealth is not possession but enjoyment.

What are all these years made for? and now another winter comes, so much like the last? Can't we satisfy the beggars once for all? Have you got in your wood for this winter? What else have you got in? Of what use a great fire on the hearth & a con-founded little fire in the heart? Are you prepared to make a deci-sive campaign—to pay for your costly tuition—to pay for the suns of past summers—for happiness & unhappiness lavished upon you?

Does not Time go by swifter than the swiftest equine trot-ter or racker?[4]

---

*Eagleswood again all cut off! [Thoreau's note, referring to the letterhead.]

Stir up Brown— Remind him of his duties, which outrun the date & span of Worcester's years past & to come. Tell him to be sure that he is on the Main Street, however narrow it may be—& to have a lit sign, visible by night as well as by day.

Are they not patient waiters—they who wait for us? But even they shall not be losers.

Dec. 7

That Walt Whitman, of whom I wrote to you, is the most interesting fact to me at present. I have just read his 2nd edition[5] (which he gave me) and it has done me more good than any reading for a long time. Perhaps I remember best the poem of Walt Whitman an American & the Sun Down Poem.[6] There are 2 or 3 pieces in the book which are disagreeable to say the least, simply sensual. He does not celebrate love at all. It is as if the beasts spoke. I think that men have not been ashamed of themselves without reason. No doubt, there have always been dens where such deeds were unblushingly recited, and it is no merit to compete with their inhabitants. But even on this side, he has spoken more truth than any American or modern that I know. I have found his poem exhilarating encouraging. As for its sensuality,—& it may turn out to be less sensual than it appeared—I do not so much wish that those parts were not written, as that men & women were so pure that they could read them without harm, that is, without understanding them. One woman told me that no woman could read it as if a man could read what a woman could not. Of course Walt Whitman can communicate to us no experience, and if we are shocked, whose experience is it that we are reminded of?

On the whole it sounds to me very brave & American after whatever deductions. I do not believe that all the sermons so called that have been preached in this land put together are equal to it for preaching—

We ought to rejoice greatly in him. He occasionally suggests something a little more than human. You can't confound him with the other inhabitants of Brooklyn or New York. How they must shudder when they read him! He is awfully good.

To be sure I sometimes feel a little imposed on. By his heartiness & broad generalities he puts me into a liberal frame of mind prepared to see wonders[7]—as it were sets me upon a hill or in the midst of a plain—stirs me well up, and then—throws in a thousand of brick. Though rude & sometimes ineffectual, it is a great primitive poem,—an alarum or trumpet-note ringing through the American camp. Wonderfully like the Orientals, too, considering that when I asked him if he had read them, he answered, "No: tell me about them."

I did not get far in conversation with him,—two more being present,—and among the few things which I chanced to say, I remember that one was, in answer to him as representing America, that I did not think much of America or of politics, and so on, which may have been somewhat of a damper to him.

Since I have seen him, I find that I am not disturbed by any brag or egoism in his book. He may turn out the least of a braggart of all, having a better right to be confident.

He is a great fellow.

➤ Letter Thirty-one

December 31, 1856, Wednesday; Concord, Massachusetts

Thoreau had delivered "Walking, or the Wild" in the basement vestry of the Congregational Church in Amherst, New Hampshire, on Thursday, December 16, noting in his journal afterward that he trusted his lecture "helped to undermine" that orthodox establishment. He had spent the two days previous to writing this letter in the field surveying the large farm of Davis Elwell near the confluence of the Sudbury and Assabet Rivers, a task he completed the following day.

Concord, December 31, 1856.

Mr. Blake,—

I think it will not be worth the while for me to come to Worcester to lecture at all this year. It will be better to wait till I am—perhaps unfortunately—more in that line. My writing has not taken the shape of lectures, and therefore I should be obliged to read one of three or four old lectures, the best of which I have read to some of your auditors before. I carried that one which I call "Walking, or the Wild," to Amherst, N.H., the evening of that cold Thursday, and I am to read another at Fitchburg, February 3. I am simply their hired man. This will probably be the extent of my lecturing hereabouts.

I must depend on meeting Mr. Wasson[1] some other time.

Perhaps it always costs me more than it comes to to lecture before a promiscuous audience. It is an irreparable injury done to my modesty even,—I become so indurated.

O solitude! obscurity! meanness! I never triumph so as when I have the least success in my neighbor's eyes. The lecturer gets fifty dollars a night; but what becomes of his winter?

What consolation will it be hereafter to have fifty thousand dollars for living in the world? I should like not to exchange *any* of my life for money.[2]

These, you may think, are reasons for not lecturing, when you have no great opportunity. It is even so, perhaps. I could lecture on dry oak leaves;[3] I could, but who could hear me? If I were to try it on any large audience, I fear it would be no gain to them, and a positive loss to me. I should have behaved rudely toward my rustling friends.

I am surveying instead of lecturing, at present. Let me have a skimming from your "pan of unwrinkled cream."[4]

H. D. T.

☙ Letter Thirty-two

February 6, 1857, Friday; Concord, Massachusetts

Contrary to his statement in the previous letter, Thoreau delivered "Walking, or the Wild," not "another" lecture, in Fitchburg, Massachusetts, on February 3. He had delivered an earlier version of the lecture in Worcester on May 31, 1851, but had "divided it into two" separate lectures, one on "Walking," the other on "The Wild," in the weeks after the publication of *Walden*.

Concord Feb. 6th 57

Mr. Blake,

I will come to you on Friday Feb. 13th with that lecture. You may call it "The Wild"—or "Walking" or both—whichever you choose. I told Brown that it had not been much altered since I read it in Worcester, but now I think of it, much of it must have been new to you, because, having since divided it into two, I am able to read what before I omitted. Nevertheless, I should like to have it understood by those whom it concerns, that I am invited to read in public (if it be so) what I have already read, in part, to a private audience.

Henry D. Thoreau.

⚛ *Letter Thirty-three*

April 17, 1857, Friday; Concord, Massachusetts

The abolitionist fighter John Brown (1800–1859) visited Concord in March 1857 during a tour to raise funds for his military efforts in Kansas. He dined at the Thoreau family table, and Thoreau spoke with him at some length about his (Brown's) childhood, young manhood, and the Battle of Black Jack in Kansas the previous June. Thoreau heard him lecture in the Concord Town Hall and donated a small sum to Brown's cause. Thoreau had spent two full weeks at Ricketson's house in New Bedford, leaving Concord on April 2 without having informed Blake, who came to visit while Thoreau was away.

Concord Ap. 17th 1857

Mr Blake,

I returned from New Bedford night before last. I met Alcott there & learned from him that probably you had gone to Concord. I am very sorry that I missed you. I had expected you earlier, & at last thought that I should get back before you came, but I ought to have notified you of my absence. However, it would have been too late, after I had made up my mind to go. I hope you lost nothing by going a little round.

I took out the Celtis seeds[1] at your request, at the time we spoke of them, and left them in the chamber on some shelf or other. If you have found them, very well; if you have not found them, very well; but tell Hale[2] of it, if you see him.

My mother says that you & Brown & Rogers[3] & Wasson (titles left behind) talk of "coming down on" me some day. Do not fail to come one & all, and within a week or two, if possible, else I *may* be gone again. Give me a short notice, and then come

& spend a day on Concord River — or say that you will come if it is fair, unless you are confident of bringing fair weather with you. Come & be Concord, as I have been Worcestered.

Perhaps you came nearer to me for not finding me at home, for trains of thought the more connect when trains of cars do not. If I had actually met you, you would have gone again, but now I have not yet dismissed you.

I hear what you say about personal relations with joy. It is as if you were to say, I value the best & finest part of you, & not the worst. I can even endure your very near & real approach, & prefer it to a shake of the hand. This intercourse is not subject to time or distance.

I have a very long new and faithful letter from Cholmonde-ley[4] which I wish to show you. He speaks of sending me more books!!

If I were with you now I could tell you much of Rickerson, and my visit to New Bedford, but I do not know how it will be by & by. I should like to have you meet R[5]—who is the frank-est man I know. Alcott & he get along very well together.

Channing[6] has returned to Concord with me, probably for a short visit only.

Consider this a business letter, which you know *counts* nothing in the game we play.

Remember me particularly to Brown.

✺ Letter Thirty-four

June 6, 1857, Saturday; Concord, Massachusetts

Thoreau left for the Cape with Channing on June 12 and, as he mentions in the next letter, returned June 22. It was to be his last visit there.

Concord, June 6, 1857, 3 p.m.

Mr. Blake,—

I have just got your note, but I am sorry to say that this very morning I sent a note to Channing, stating that I would go with him to Cape Cod next week on an excursion which we have been talking of for some time. If there were time to communicate with you, I should ask you to come to Concord on Monday, before I go; but as it is, I must wait till I come back, which I think will be about ten days hence. I do not like this delay, but there seems to be a fate in it. Perhaps Mr. Wasson will be well enough to come by that time. I will notify you of my return, and shall depend on seeing you all.

☙ Letter Thirty-five

On Monday morning, June 29, Thoreau and Blake went boating on the Assabet River in Concord, apparently unaccompanied by others. Probably he italicized "Mediterranean" to call attention to the word's etymology: "in the middle of land" or "surrounded by land." Cholmondeley's long letter to Thoreau dated May 26 has not yet been published; it contains, among other matters, his responses to the four books Thoreau sent (see note 12 to Letter 26).

Concord Tuesday Morning June 23d 1857

Mr Blake,

I returned from Cape Cod last evening, and now take the first opportunity to invite you men of Worcester to this quiet *Mediterranean* shore. Can you come this week on Friday or next Monday? I mention the earliest days on which I suppose you can be ready. If more convenient name some other time *within ten days*. I shall be rejoiced to see you, and to act the part of skipper in the contemplated voyage. I have just got another letter from Cholmondeley, which may interest you somewhat.

H. D. T.

⁂ Letter Thirty-six

August 18, 1857, Tuesday; Concord, Massachusetts

Thoreau hosted Theo Brown and Seth Rogers in Concord on July 4. On July 11 he wrote letters to Eben J. Loomis (1818–1912), a friend in nearby Cambridge, and to his cousin George Thatcher, who lived in Bangor, Maine, inquiring whether they would like to accompany him on an excursion into the woods of Maine. In his letter to Thatcher he mentioned a friend who wanted to go as well but who had "neither woodcraft nor strength enough." That friend was Blake, whom one suspects was upset with Thoreau for failing to invite him along. In any case, neither Loomis nor Thatcher was able to accompany Thoreau on such short notice, but he was able to get Edward Hoar (1823–1893), the son of Concord's leading citizen, Judge Samuel Hoar (1778–1856), to make the trip with him. When the two reached Maine they hired Joe Polis (1809–1884) of Oldtown as their guide. The trip lasted from July 20 to August 8. It was to be Thoreau's final excursion to the Maine woods; his account of it was published posthumously as the third chapter of *The Maine Woods*.

H. G. O. Blake
Worcester Mass

Concord Aug. 18th 1857.

Mr Blake,

XVth ly[1]

It seems to me that you need some absorbing pursuit. It does not matter much what it is, so it be honest. Such employment will be favorable to your development in more characteristic and important directions. You know there must be impulse enough for steerage way,[2] though it be not toward your port—to prevent your drifting helplessly—on to rocks or shoals. Some sails are set for this purpose only.[3] There is the large fleet of scholars & men of science, for instance, always to be seen standing off and on on every coast, and saved thus from running on to reefs, who will at last run into their proper havens, we trust.

It is a pity you were not here with Brown and Rogers. I think that in this case, *for a rarity,* the more the merrier.

You perceived that I did not entertain the idea of our going together to Maine on such an excursion as I had planned. The more I thought of it, the more imprudent it appeared to me. I did think to have written to you before going, though not to propose your going also, but I went at last very suddenly, and could only have written a business letter, if I had tried, when there was no business to be accomplished.

I have now returned, and think I have had a quite profitable journey, chiefly from associating with an intelligent Indian.[4] My companion, Edward Hoar, also found his account in it, though he suffered considerably from being obliged to carry unusual loads over wet & rough "carries,"—in one instance five miles through a swamp, where the water was frequently up to our knees & the fallen timber higher than our heads. He went over the ground three times, not being able to carry all his load at once. This prevented his ascending Ktadn.[5] Our best nights were those when it rained the hardest on account of the mosquitoes. I speak of these things, which were not unexpected, merely to account for my not inviting you.

Having returned, I flatter myself that the world appears in some respects a little larger, and not, as usual, smaller & shallower, for having extended my range. I have made a short excursion into the new world which the Indian dwells in, or is. He begins where we leave off. It is worth the while to detect new faculties in man—he is so much the more divine,—and anything that fairly excites our admiration expands us. The Indian who can find his way so wonderfully in the woods possesses so much intelligence which the white man does not, and it increases my own capacity, as well as faith, to observe it. I rejoice to find that intelligence flows in other channels than I knew— It redeems for me portions of what seemed brutish before.

It is a great satisfaction to find that your oldest convictions are permanent. With regard to essentials I have never had occasion to change my mind. The aspect of the world varies from year to year, as the landscape is differently clothed, but I find that the *truth* is still *true*, & I never regret any emphasis which it may have inspired. Ktadn is there still, but much more surely my old conviction is there, resting with more than mountain breadth & weight on the world, the source still of fertilizing streams, & affording glorious views from its summit, if I can get up to it again. As the *mts.* still stand on the plain, and far more unchangeable & permanent, stand still grouped around, farther or nearer to my maturer eye, the ideas which I have entertained—the everlasting teats[6] from which we draw our nourishment.

H. D. T.

⁂ Letter Thirty-seven

November 16, 1857, Monday; Concord, Massachusetts

Very likely Blake undertook his solitary journey to the White
Mountains in part because of the suggestion implicit in the previous letter—and made quite explicit in this letter—that he would not have been
up to the rigors of the Maine excursion of July–August. Throughout the
summer of 1857 the American economy had slowed noticeably, and in
early September the failure of several New York banks precipitated a full-
scale financial panic. Banks that remained solvent reacted to the panic by
suspending specie payments. This dramatic economic downturn, afterward called the Depression of 1857, was the worst since the Depression
of 1837. Sometime after returning from Maine, Thoreau grew a full
beard, which he kept for the remainder of his life.

Concord, November 16, 1857.

Mr Blake,—

You have got the start again. It was I that owed you a letter
or two, if I mistake not.

They make a great ado nowadays about hard times; but I
think that the community generally, ministers and all, take a
wrong view of the matter, though some of the ministers preaching according to a formula may pretend to take a right one.
This general failure, both private and public, is rather occasion
for rejoicing, as reminding us whom we have at the helm,—that
justice is always done. If our merchants did not most of them
fail, and the banks too, my faith in the old laws of the world
would be staggered. The statement that ninety-six in a hundred
doing such business surely break down[1] is perhaps the sweetest
fact that statistics have revealed,—exhilarating as the fragrance

of sallows in spring. Does it not say somewhere, "The Lord reigneth, let the earth rejoice"?[2] If thousands are thrown out of employment, it suggests that they were not well employed. Why don't they take the hint? It is not enough to be industrious; so are the ants. What are you industrious about?

The merchants and company have long laughed at transcendentalism, higher laws, etc., crying, "None of your moonshine,"[3] as if they were anchored to something not only definite, but sure and permanent. If there was any institution which was presumed to rest on a solid and secure basis, and more than any other represented this boasted common sense, prudence, and practical talent, it was the bank; and now those very banks are found to be mere reeds shaken by the wind.[4] Scarcely one in the land has kept its promise. It would seem as if you only need live forty years in any age of this world, to see its most promising government become the government of Kansas,[5] and banks nowhere. Not merely the Brook Farm and Fourierite communities,[6] but now the community generally has failed. But there is the moonshine still, serene, beneficent, and unchanged. Hard times, I say, have this value, among others, that they show us what such promises are worth,—where the *sure* banks are. I heard some merchant praised the other day because he had paid some of his debts, though it took nearly all he had (why, I've done as much as that myself many times, and a little more), and then gone to board.[7] What if he has? I hope he's got a good boarding-place, and can pay for it. It's not everybody that can. However, in my opinion, it is cheaper to keep house,[8]—*i.e.*, if you don't keep too big a one.

Men will tell you sometimes that "money's hard." That

shows it was not made to eat, I say. Only think of a man in this new world, in his log cabin, in the midst of a corn and potato patch, with a sheepfold on one side, talking about money being hard! So are flints hard; there is no alloy in them. What has that to do with his raising his food, cutting his wood (or breaking it), keeping in-doors when it rains, and, if need be, spinning and weaving his clothes? Some of those who sank with the steamer the other day[9] found out that money was *heavy* too. Think of a man's priding himself on this kind of wealth, as if it greatly enriched him. As if one struggling in mid-ocean with a bag of gold on his back should gasp out, "I am worth a hundred thousand dollars." I see them struggling just as ineffectually on dry land, nay, even more hopelessly, for, in the former case, rather than sink, they will finally let the bag go; but in the latter they are pretty sure to hold and go down with it. I see them swimming about in their great coats, collecting their rents, really *getting their dues*, drinking bitter draughts which only increase their thirst, becoming more and more water-logged, till finally they sink plumb down to the bottom. But enough of this.

Have you ever read Ruskin's books?[10] If not, I would recommend you to try the second and third volumes (not parts) of his "Modern Painters." I am now reading the fourth, and have read most of his other books lately. They are singularly good and encouraging, though not without crudeness and bigotry. The themes in the volumes referred to are Infinity, Beauty, Imagination, Love of Nature, etc.,—all treated in a very living manner. I am rather surprised by them. It is remarkable that these things should be said with reference to painting chiefly, rather than literature. The "Seven Lamps of Architecture," too, is made of good stuff; but, as I remember, there is too much about art in it for me and the Hottentots.[11] We want to know about matters and things in general. Our house is as yet a hut.

You must have been enriched by your solitary walk over the mountains.[12] I suppose that I feel the same awe when on their summits that many do on entering a church. To see what kind of earth that is on which you have a house and garden somewhere, perchance! It is equal to the lapse of many years. You must ascend a mountain to learn your relation to matter, and so to your own body, for *it* is at home there, though *you* are not. It might have been composed there, and will have no farther to go to return to dust there, than in your garden; but your spirit inevitably comes away, and brings your body with it, if it lives. Just as awful really, and as glorious, is your garden. See how I can play with my fingers! They are the funniest companions I have ever found. Where did they come from? What strange control I have over them! *Who* am I?[13] What are they?—those little peaks—call them Madison, Jefferson, Lafayette.[14] What is *the matter*? *My* fingers ten, I say. Why, erelong, they may form the top-most crystal of Mount Washington. I go up there to see my body's cousins. There are some fingers, toes, bowels, etc., that I take an interest in, and therefore I am interested in all their relations.

Let me suggest a theme for you: to state to yourself precisely and completely what that walk over the mountains amounted to for you,—returning to this essay again and again, until you are satisfied that all that was important in your experience is in it. Give this good reason to yourself for having gone over the mountains, for mankind is ever going over a mountain. Don't suppose that you can tell it precisely the first dozen times you try, but at 'em again, especially when, after a sufficient pause, you suspect that you are touching the heart or summit of the matter, reiterate your blows there, and account for the mountain to yourself. Not that the story need be long, but it will take a long while to make it short. It did not take very long to get over the mountain, you thought; but have you got over it indeed? If you have been to the top of Mount Washington, let me ask, what did you find there? That is the way they prove witnesses, you know. Going up there and being blown on is nothing. We never do much climbing while we are there, but we eat our luncheon, etc., very much as at home. It is after we get home that we really go over the mountain, if ever. What did the mountain say? What did the mountain do?

I keep a mountain anchored off eastward a little way, which I ascend in my dreams both awake and asleep. Its broad base spreads over a village or two, which do not know it; neither does it know them, nor do I when I ascend it. I can see its general outline as plainly now in my mind as that of Wachusett. I do not invent in the least, but state exactly what I see. I find that I go up it when I am light-footed and earnest. It ever smokes like an altar with its sacrifice. I am not aware that a single villager frequents it or knows of it. I keep this mountain to ride instead of a horse.

Do you not mistake about seeing Moosehead Lake from Mount Washington? That must be about one hundred and twenty miles distant, or nearly twice as far as the Atlantic, which last some doubt if they can see thence. Was it not Umbagog?[15]

Dr. Solger[16] has been lecturing in the vestry in this town on Geography, to Sanborn's scholars, for several months past, at five P. M. Emerson and Alcott have been to hear him. I was surprised when the former asked me, the other day, if I was not going to hear Dr. Solger. What, to be sitting in a meeting-house cellar at that time of day, when you might possibly be outdoors! I never thought of such a thing. What was the sun made for? If he does not prize daylight, I do. Let him lecture to owls and dormice. He must be a wonderful lecturer indeed who can keep me indoors at such an hour, when the night is coming in which no man can walk.[17]

Are you in want of amusement nowadays? Then play a little at the game of getting a living. There never was anything equal to it. Do it temperately, though, and don't sweat. Don't let this secret out, for I have a design against the Opera.[18] OPERA!! Pass along the exclamations, devil.[19]

Now is the time to become conversant with your wood-pile (this comes under Work for the Month), and be sure you put some warmth into it by your mode of getting it. Do not consent to be passively warmed. An intense degree of that is the hotness that is threatened. But a positive warmth within can withstand the fiery furnace, as the vital heat of a living man can withstand the heat that cooks meat.

ᴅᴀᴡ Letter Thirty-eight

June 1, 1858, Tuesday; Concord, Massachusetts

On the way to New York City in late May to conduct business relating to his family's graphite supply firm, Thoreau stayed overnight at Blake's in Worcester (May 22) and enjoyed a long outing the next day with Blake, Brown, and Rogers. The morning after writing this letter he met Blake at the rail depot in Fitchburg, Massachusetts, and the two men continued on together to Troy, New Hampshire, from which they walked to Mount Monadnock, five miles to the east. They camped two nights on the mountain, walked the twelve miles to the train station at Winchendon, Massachusetts, the morning of June 4, and returned to their respective homes. Thoreau's essay "Chesuncook" began appearing serially in the June issue of the *Atlantic Monthly*, but publication was halted after the August issue when the editor, James Russell Lowell (1819–1891), dropped without Thoreau's permission what he regarded as the heretical sentence "It [the pine tree] is as immortal as I am, and perchance will go to as high a heaven, there to tower above me still."

Concord Tuesday 4 *pm* June 1st 1858

Mr Blake—

It looks as if it might rain tomorrow; therefore this is to inform you—if you have not left Worcester on account of rain, that if the weather prevents my starting tomorrow, I intend to start on Thursday morning—i.e. if it is not decidedly rainy— or something more than a shower, and I trust that I shall meet you at Troy as agreed on.

H. D. T.

☙ *Letter Thirty-nine*

June 29, 1858, Tuesday; Concord, Massachusetts

As he explains in Letter 40, Thoreau mailed this letter to Blake's home in Worcester, but Blake appears to have been visiting his in-laws in Sterling, Massachusetts, and therefore did not receive the letter in a timely fashion.

Concord, June 29, 1858, 8 A.M.

Mr. Blake,—

Edward Hoar and I propose to start for the White Mountains in a covered wagon, with one horse, on the morning of Thursday the 1st of July, intending to explore the mountain tops botanically, and camp on them at least several times. Will you take a seat in the wagon with us? Mr. Hoar prefers to hire the horse and wagon himself. Let us hear by express, as soon as you can, whether you will join us here by the earliest train Thursday morning, or Wednesday night. Bring your map of the mountains, and as much *provision* for the road as you can,— hard bread, sugar, tea, meat, etc.,—for we intend to live like gypsies; also, a blanket and some thick clothes for the mountain top.

⚞ *Letter Forty*

July 1, 1858, Thursday; Concord, Massachusetts

Apparently delayed because they had not heard from Blake, Hoar and Thoreau left Concord in their private carriage on July 2. The night of July 4 they camped near Senter (usually Center) Harbor, New Hampshire, a village at the northern extremity of Lake Winnepesaukee. On July 7 they stopped by the Glen House below Pinkham Notch, left a note there for Blake, and ascended Mount Washington, joined by one William H. H. Wentworth, whom Hoar had hired on as a packer. The following afternoon, as Thoreau reported in his journal, "we heard, as we thought, a faint shout, and it occurred to me that Blake . . . might possibly be looking for me; but soon Wentworth decided that it must be a bear, for they make a noise like a woman in distress. He has caught many of them. Nevertheless, we shouted in return and waved a light coat on the meadow. After an hour or two had elapsed, we heard the voice again, nearer, and saw two men, and I went up the stream to meet Blake and Brown, wet, ragged, and bloody with black flies." The next morning Thoreau sprained his ankle in Tuckerman Ravine and had to lay up the remainder of that day and the next. The five-man party continued botanizing on and around Mount Washington until July 16, when Thoreau, Hoar, Blake, and Brown headed home, arriving in Concord at noon on July 19. A few of the incidents that took place during this trip are interestingly echoed in Letter 41.

Concord, July 1, 1858

July 1st. Last Monday evening Mr. Edward Hoar said that he thought of going to the White Mountains. I remarked casually that I should like to go well enough if I could afford it. Where-upon he declared that if I would go with him, he would hire a horse and wagon, so that the ride would cost me nothing, and we would explore the mountain tops *botanically,* camping on them many nights. The next morning I suggested you and Brown's accompanying us in another wagon, and we could all camp and cook, gypsy-like, along the way,—or, perhaps, if the horse could draw us, you would like to bear half the expense of the horse and wagon, and take a seat with us. He liked either proposition, but said, that if you would take a seat with us, he would prefer to hire the horse and wagon himself. You could contribute something else if you pleased. Supposing that Brown would be confined, I wrote to you accordingly, by *express* on Tuesday morning, *via* Boston, stating that we should start to-day, suggesting provision, thick clothes, etc., and asking for an answer; but I have not received one. I have just heard that you *may* be at Sterling, and now write to say that we shall still be glad if you will join us at Senter Harbor, where we expect to be next Monday morning. In any case, will you please direct a letter to us there *at once*?

ᔷ Letter Forty-one

January 1, 1859, Saturday; Concord, Massachusetts

In late November Cholmondeley had mailed Thoreau a letter from Montreal stating that he would be visiting Boston before heading to the West Indies for the winter, whither he asked Thoreau to join him. Later, after Cholmondeley's arrival, he suggested to Thoreau that they explore the valley of the Amazon together, but Thoreau demurred once again, telling his English friend, "I think I had better stay in Concord." Thoreau's two most fervent admirers outside of his family, Blake and Ricketson, met one another and apparently did not hit it off particularly well. They were, in fact, very different personalities—Blake extremely serious and highly idealistic, Ricketson remarkably self-absorbed and literal-minded. Emerson and his compeers in the Saturday Club, had they stuck to their routine of meeting the last Saturday of the month, would have convened at the Parker House in Boston on Christmas Day. It would appear that Emerson attempted to attract Thoreau to the meeting.

Concord, January 1, 1859.

Mr. Blake,—

It may interest you to hear that Cholmondeley has been this way again, *via* Montreal and Lake Huron, going to the West Indies, or rather to Weiss-nicht-wo,[1] whither he urges me to accompany him. He is rather more demonstrative than before, and, on the whole, what would be called "a good fellow,"—is a man of principle, and quite reliable, but very peculiar. I have been to New Bedford with him, to show him a whaling town and Ricketson. I was glad to hear that you had called on R. How did you like him? I suspect that you did not see one another fairly.

I have lately got back to that glorious society called Solitude, where we meet our friends continually, and can imagine the outside world also to be peopled. Yet some of my acquaintance would fain hustle me into the almshouse for *the sake of society,* as if I were pining for that diet, when I seem to myself a most befriended man, and find constant employment. However, they do not believe a word I say. They have got a club, the handle of which is in the Parker House at Boston,[2] and with this they beat me from time to time, expecting to make me tender or minced meat, so fit for a club to dine off.

> "Hercules with his club
> The Dragon did drub;
> But More of More Hall,
> With nothing at all,
> He slew the Dragon of Wantley."[3]

Ah! that More of More Hall knew what fair play was. Channing, who wrote to me about it once, brandishing the club vigorously (being set on by another, probably), says *now,* seriously, that he is sorry to find by my letters that I am "absorbed in politics," and adds, begging my pardon for his plainness, "Beware of an extraneous life!" and so he does his duty, and washes his hands of me. I tell him that it is as if he should say to the sloth, that fellow that creeps so slowly along a tree, and cries *ai* from time to time, "Beware of dancing!"

The doctors are all agreed that I am suffering from want of society. Was never a case like it. First, I did not know that I was suffering at all. Secondly, as an Irishman might say, I had thought it was indigestion of the society I got. It is indispensable that I should take a dose of Lowell & Agassiz & Woodman.[4]

As for the Parker House, I went there once, when the Club was away, but I found it hard to see through the cigar smoke, and men were deposited about in chairs over the marble floor, as thick as legs of bacon in a smoke-house. It was all smoke, and no salt, Attic[5] or other. The only room in Boston which I visit with alacrity is the Gentlemen's Room at the Fitchburg Depot,[6] where I wait for the cars, sometimes for two hours, in order to get out of town. It is a paradise to the Parker House, for no smoking is allowed, and there is far more retirement. A large and respectable club of us hire it (Town and Country Club),[7] and I am pretty sure to find some one there whose face is set the same way as my own.

My last essay, on which I am still engaged, is called Autumnal Tints.[8] I do not know how readable (*i.e.*, by me to others) it will be.

I met Mr. James the other night at Emerson's, at an Alcottian conversation,[9] at which, however, Alcott did not talk much, being disturbed by James's opposition. The latter is a hearty man enough, with whom you can differ very satisfactorily, on account of both his doctrines and his good temper. He utters *quasi* philanthropic dogmas in a metaphysic dress; but they are for all practical purposes very crude. He charges society with all the crime committed, and praises the criminal for committing it. But I think that all the remedies he suggests out of his head—for he goes no farther, hearty as he is—would leave us about where we are now. For, of course, it is not by a gift of turkeys on Thanksgiving Day that he proposes to convert the criminal, but by a true sympathy with each one,—with him, among the rest, who lyingly tells the world from the gallows that he has never been treated kindly by a single mortal since he was born.[10] But it is not so easy a thing to sympathize with another, though you may have the best disposition to do it. There is Dobson[11] over the hill. Have not you and I and all the world been trying, ever since he was born, to sympathize with him? (as doubtless he with us), and yet we have got no farther than to send him to the House of Correction once at least; and he, on the other hand, as I hear, has sent us to another place several times.[12] This is the real state of things, as I understand it, at least so far as James's remedies go. We are now, alas! exercising what charity we actually have, and new laws would not give us any more. But, perchance, we might make some improvements in the House of Correction. You and I are Dobson; what will James do for us?

Have you found at last in your wanderings a place where the solitude is sweet?

What mountain are you camping on nowadays? Though I had a good time at the mountains, I confess that the journey did not bear any fruit that I know of. I did not expect it would. The mode of it was not simple and adventurous enough. You must first have made an infinite demand, and not unreasonably, but after a corresponding outlay, have an all-absorbing purpose, and at the same time that your feet bear you hither and thither, travel much more in imagination.

To let the mountains slide,—live at home like a traveler. It should not be in vain that these things are shown us from day to day. Is not each withered leaf that I see in my walks something which I have traveled to find?—traveled, who can tell how far? What a fool he must be who thinks that his El Dorado[13] is anywhere but where he lives!

We are always, methinks, in some kind of ravine, though our bodies may walk the smooth streets of Worcester. Our souls (I use this word for want of a better) are ever perched on its rocky sides, overlooking that lowland. (What a more than Tuckerman's Ravine[14] is the body itself, in which the "soul" is encamped, when you come to look into it! However, eagles always have chosen such places for their eyries.)

Thus is it ever with your fair cities of the plain.[15] Their streets may be paved with silver and gold, and six carriages roll abreast in them, but the real *homes* of the citizens are in the Tuckerman's Ravines which ray out from that centre into the mountains round about, one for each man, woman, and child. The masters of life have so ordered it. That is their *beau-ideal* of a country seat. There is no danger of being *tuckered* out before you get to it.

So we live in Worcester and in Concord, each man taking his exercise regularly in his ravine, like a lion in his cage, and sometimes spraining his ankle there. We have very few clear days, and a great many small plagues which keep us busy. Sometimes, I suppose, you hear a neighbor halloo (Brown, may be) and think it is a bear. Nevertheless, on the whole, we think it very grand and exhilarating, this ravine life. It is a capital advantage withal, living so high, the excellent drainage of that city of God.[16] Routine is but a shallow and insignificant sort of ravine, such as the ruts are, the conduits of puddles. But these ravines are the source of mighty streams, precipitous, icy, savage, as they are, haunted by bears and loup-cerviers;[17] there are born not only Sacos and Amazons,[18] but prophets who will redeem the world. The at last smooth and fertilizing water at which nations drink and navies supply themselves begins with melted glaciers, and burst thunder-spouts. Let us pray that, if we are not flowing through some Mississippi valley which we fertilize,—and it is not likely we are,—we may know ourselves shut in between grim and mighty mountain walls amid the clouds, falling a thousand feet in a mile, through dwarfed fir and spruce, over the rocky insteps of slides, being exercised in our minds, and so developed.

✒ Letter Forty-two

January 19 and 29, 1859, Wednesday and Saturday;
Concord, Massachusetts

Thoreau's father, John Thoreau Sr., had been ill for quite some time, which circumstance had increasingly compelled Thoreau to handle matters relating to the family's business. Those matters fell wholly upon his shoulders when his father died on February 3. In the letter to which Thoreau responds here, Blake once again suggested that his friend deliver "What Shall It Profit" a second time in Worcester, either overlooking the remark in Letter 41 about "Autumnal Tints" or assuming Thoreau would not have that nascent lecture ready in good time. Blake also appears to have mentioned in his letter having written a paper about his "adventures in the Ravine." Tuckerman Ravine is doubtless meant, and the paper was almost certainly the result of Blake's compliance with the suggestion in Letter 37 that he "state to [himself] precisely and completely what [his solitary] walk over the mountains amounted to" for him.

Concord, January 19, 1859.

Mr. Blake,—

If I could have given a favorable report as to the skating, I should have answered you earlier. About a week before you wrote there was good skating; there is now none. As for the lecture, I shall be glad to come. I cannot now say when, but I will let you know, I think within a week or ten days at most, and will then leave you a week clear to make the arrangements in. I will bring something else than "What shall it profit a Man?" My father is very sick, and has been for a long time, so that there is the more need of me at home. This occurs to me, even when contemplating so short an excursion as to Worcester.

I want very much to see or hear your account of your adventures in the Ravine, and I trust I shall do so when I come to Worcester. Cholmondeley has been here again, returning from Virginia (for he went no farther south) to Canada; and will go thence to Europe, he thinks, in the spring, and never ramble any more. (January 29). I am expecting daily that my father will die, therefore I cannot leave home at present. I will write you again within ten days.

﹥ Letter Forty-three

February 7, 1859, Monday; Concord, Massachusetts

The delay occasioned by his father's illness and death enabled Thoreau to complete enough of "Autumnal Tints" to read a portion of it by February 15, but in a letter to Ricketson on February 12 he mentions that he was "going to Worcester to read a parlor lecture on the 22nd." He did indeed read the "Autumnal Tints" extracts in Worcester on that date, either at Blake's school at 1 Warren Block on Pearl Street or in Blake's home at 3 Bowdoin Street. As explained in note 3 to Letter 31 above, "Autumnal Tints" grew over the months into a much larger project that Thoreau called *The Fall of the Leaf*.

Concord Feb. 7th 1859

Mr. Blake,

I will come and read you an extract from "Autumnal Tints," on Tuesday the 15th, of this month, if that is agreeable to you,—leaving here probably at noon. Perhaps you had better acknowledge the receipt of this.

H. D. T.

🌿 *Letter Forty-four*

September 26, 1859, Monday; Concord, Massachusetts

The Thoreau family business thrived throughout the 1850s, and with the death of his father Thoreau was left to run it himself, which reduced dramatically the free time he had become accustomed to enjoying over the years. Blake and Brown visited him in Concord on April 28, and the following month he again met John Brown, who once more visited Concord from Kansas. As he had done during his previous visit, Brown spoke at the Concord Town Hall, but this time Thoreau was considerably more impressed with Brown than he had been before. Doubtless inspired by Thoreau's accounts of Cape Cod, Blake visited the Cape himself but clearly found the place not so much to his liking.

Concord Sep. 26th 1859

Mr Blake,

I am not sure that I am in a fit mood to write to you, for I feel & think rather too much like a business man, having some very irksome affairs to attend to these months and years on account of my family. This is the way I am serving King Admetus[1]—confound him! If it were not for my relations I would let the wolves prey on his flocks to their bellies' content. Such fellows you have to deal with! herdsmen of some other king, or of the same, who tell no tale, but in the sense of counting their flocks, & then lie drunk under a hedge. How is your grist ground?— Not by some murmuring stream, while you lie dreaming on the bank, but, it seems, you must take hold with your hands & shove the wheel round. You can't depend on streams, poor feeble things! You can't depend on worlds, left to themselves, but you've got to oil them & goad them along. In short, you've got to carry on 2 farms at once, the farm on the earth, and the farm in your mind. Those Crimean and Italian battles[2] were mere boy's play—they are the scrapes into which truants get. But what a battle a man must fight everywhere to maintain his standing army[3] of thoughts, & march with them in orderly array through the always hostile country! How many enemies there are to sane thinking! Every soldier has succumbed to them before he enlists for those other battles. Men may sit in chambers, seemingly safe & sound, & yet despair, and turn out at last only hollowness & dust within, like a Dead-sea apple.[4] A standing army of numerous, brave, & well-disciplined thoughts, & you at the head of them, marching straight to your goal!— How to bring this about is the problem, & Scotts' Tactics[5] will not help you to it. Think of a poor fellow begirt only with a sword-belt, & no such staff of athletic thoughts! his brains rattling as he walks, and *talks!*— These are your Pretorian guard.[6]

It is easy enough to maintain a family, or a state, but it is hard to maintain these children of your brain (or say rather these guests that trust to enjoy your hospitality), they make such great demands; and yet he who does only the former, and loses the power to *think* originally, or as only he ever can, fails miserably. Keep up the fires of thought and all will go well.

Zouaves?— Pish![7] How you can overrun a country, climb any rampart, and carry any fortress, with an army of alert thoughts!—thoughts that send their bullets home to heaven's door—with which you can *take* the whole world, without paying for it, or robbing any body. See the conquering hero comes! You *fail* in your thoughts, or you *prevail* in your thoughts only.

Provided you *think* well, the heavens falling, or the earth gaping, will be music for you to march by. No foe can ever see you, or you him; you cannot so much as *think* of him. Swords have no edges, bullets no penetration, for such a contest. In your mind must be a liquor which will dissolve the world whenever it is dropt in it. There is no universal solvent but this, & all things together cannot saturate it. It will hold the universe in solution, & yet be as translucent as ever. The vast machine may indeed roll over our toes, & we not know it, but it would rebound & be staved to pieces like an empty barrel, if it should strike fair & square, on the smallest & least angular of a man's thoughts.

You seem not to have taken Cape Cod the right way. I think that you should have persevered in walking on the beach and on the bank, even to the land's end, however soft, & so, by long knocking at Ocean's gate,[8] have gained admittance at last; better if separately, & in a storm,[9] not knowing where you would sleep by night, or eat by day. Then you should have given a day to the sand behind Provincetown,[10] & ascended the hills there, & been blown on considerably. I hope that you like to remember the journey better than you did to make it.

I have been confined at home all this year, but I am not aware that I have grown any rustier than was to be expected. One while I explored the bottom of the river[11] pretty extensively. I have engaged to read a lecture to Parker's society[12] on the 9th of October next.

Emerson has been seriously lame for 2 or 3 months past— Sprained his foot—& does not yet get better.[13] It has been a bad business for him—

I am off—a barberrying   H. D. T.

⇨ Letter Forty-five

October 31, 1859, Monday; Concord, Massachusetts

Blake visited Thoreau on October 13, staying overnight and joining him the next morning for a walk around Flint's Pond in Lincoln, Massachusetts, one of the towns adjoining Concord. During this month Thoreau began work on a massively ambitious project, *Wild Fruits*, wherein he planned to catalog and describe in considerable detail the complete natural history of all the naturally occurring fruits of his hometown in their order of ripening, as well as survey how humankind over the millennia had used and enjoyed each of those fruits. Unfortunately, this project was left unfinished at his death, and a reconstructed version of the incomplete project was not published until 2000. On October 19, five days after Blake returned home from his visit, the first report arrived in Concord of John Brown's raid on the federal arsenal at Harpers Ferry, Virginia (now West Virginia). Brown and twenty-one men aspired to rid the land of the iniquity of slavery by leading an insurrection and arming the slaves with weapons from the arsenal. Instead, ten of the men were killed, including two of Brown's sons; five escaped and were never caught. Brown was among the remaining six who were captured and quickly brought to trial. Thoreau's response to the initial reports was swift, decisive, unequivocal. Brown's character, if not his specific actions, must be defended at all hazards. Thoreau's journal, filled with observations about nature in the days leading up to October 19, is filled with nothing but his thoughts on the John Brown affair through the remainder of the month. As more news came to him through the Boston newspapers, particularly the reports of what Brown said to his captors as he lay wounded on the armory's engine house floor, Thoreau's indignation mounted, as did his respect for Brown's character. While the nation rowdily debated the import of this incredibly dramatic event and argued about Brown's sanity, Thoreau organized his journal comments into a lecture. When he sent word around town that he would deliver a defense of Brown, the local abolitionists responded that a defense at that time might be counterproductive. Thoreau replied, "I did not send to you for advice, but to announce that I am to speak." His lecture "A Plea for Captain John Brown," delivered in the vestry of the Unitarian Meet-inghouse in Concord on October 30, made him the first person in the country to speak out publicly in support of Brown. It was a daring, even a dangerous act, but wholly characteristic. The lecture inaugurated a gradual swaying of the public's mind in the Free States, a development that was completed eighteen months later, when many troops assembled from those states and marched southward to the song "John Brown's Body." Two days after the Concord lecture and the day after this letter to Blake, November 1, Thoreau read the lecture again, this time in one of Boston's foremost auditoriums, the Tremont Temple. The black abo-litionist orator Frederick Douglass had been scheduled to speak, but he had left hastily for Canada, fearing reprisals for his suspected involve-ment in planning Brown's raid. On October 31, probably after writing to Blake, Thoreau had received an urgent telegram from Boston asking him to stand in for Douglass. The lecture was scheduled for 7:30 p.m., but Tremont Hall was filled with 2,500 auditors at 7 p.m. Thoreau spoke for an hour and a half, giving what seems to have been one of his best performances on the lecture platform, for the newspaper reports indicate that the audience listened with "enthusiastic approval" and that Thoreau's speech was several times interrupted by applause. When Blake received this letter from Thoreau, he quickly rented Washburn Hall in Worcester's new Mechanic's Hall building on Main Street for Thursday, November 3. Higginson was not in town when the letter arrived but was returning from upstate New York, where he had gone to speak with Mrs. Brown in North Elba about persuading her husband to allow his friends in the North to rescue him from prison. (Brown, understanding that his martyrdom was far more valuable to the cause of abolition than his life, had refused offers of rescue.) The court in Virginia issued its verdict the day before Thoreau's Worcester engagement, November 2: death by hanging in one month. The next day's newspapers contained the text of John Brown's last speech to the court, a speech that many American schoolchildren throughout the latter half of the nineteenth century were required to recite from memory. Thoreau read Brown's brief speech at the close of his Worcester lecture that evening. The next day he stopped by Alcott's house in Concord and reported on both his Boston and

Worcester lectures, after which Alcott wrote in his diary, "Thoreau has good right to speak fully his mind concerning Brown, and has been the first to speak and celebrate the hero's courage and magnanimity. It is these which he discerns and praises. The men have much in common: the sturdy manliness, straight-forwardness and independence. It is well they met, and that Thoreau saw what he sets forth as no one else can."

Concord Oct 31st

Mr Blake.

I spoke to my townsmen last evening on "the character of Capt. Brown, now in the clutches of the slaveholder." I should like to speak to any company in Worcester who may wish to hear me, & will come, if only my expenses are paid.

I think that we should express ourselves at once, while Brown is alive. The sooner the better. Perhaps Higginson may like to have a meeting.

Wednesday evening would be a good time.

The people here are deeply interested in the matter.

Let me have an answer as soon as may be.

Henry D. Thoreau

P.S. I may be engaged toward the end of the week.

ᗦᗢ Letter Forty-six

May 20, 1860, Sunday; Concord, Massachusetts

Thoreau had delivered a new lecture, "Wild Apples," in Concord on February 8. It was part of *Wild Fruits*, the project he had begun working on the previous October, right around the time of Blake's last visit. Shortly after his delivery of "Wild Apples," he read the first American edition of *On the Origin of Species*, an intellectual bombshell that continues to be controversial in our time. Charles Darwin (1809–1882) had published the treatise in London the preceding October. He knew it would spark controversy, and it certainly did that. Thoreau was one of the first Americans to read the book, and because of his incredible open-mindedness and his wide reading in natural history, particularly since 1851, he was an unusually fit reader for this particular book. The final chapter contains an eloquent plea encouraging natural historians with evidence supporting the "developmental" thesis (now more popularly known as the theory of evolution) to gather and present their evidence. Thoreau responded by immediately beginning to assemble the observations on seed dispersion and forest succession scattered throughout his journal of the preceding ten and more years. As Thoreau well knew, those observations firmly, even conclusively supported one of the most critical links in Darwin's argument, the one on the geographical distribution of species. He read a paper on "The Succession of Forest Trees" in Concord on September 20, 1860. The essay was widely reprinted shortly thereafter. Regrettably, he did not live to complete his treatise *The Dispersion of Seeds*, the scattered leaves of which were not reconstructed and published until 1993 in *Faith in a Seed*. In that manuscript he eloquently sums up his thoughts on Darwin's revolutionary theory: "The development theory implies a greater vital force in nature, because it is more flexible and accommodating, and equivalent to a sort of constant new creation." Precisely the same point can be made about Thoreau's religious thought.

Concord May 20 1860

Mr Blake,

I must endeavor to pay some of my debts to you.

To begin where we left off then.

The presumption is that *we* are always the same; our opportunities & Nature herself fluctuating. Look at mankind. No great difference between two, apparently; perhaps the same height and breadth and weight; and yet to the man who sits most E.[I] this life is a weariness, routine, dust and ashes, and he drowns his imaginary cares (!) (a sort of friction among his vital organs), in a bowl. But to the man who sits most W., his *contemporary* (!), it is a field for all noble endeavors, an elysium, the dwelling place of heroes & knights. The former complains that he has a thousand affairs to attend to; but he does not realize, that his affairs, (though they may be a thousand,) and he are one.

Men & boys are learning all kinds of trades but how to make *men* of themselves. They learn to make houses, but they are not so well housed, they are not so contented in their houses, as the woodchucks in their holes. What is the use of a house if you haven't got a tolerable planet to put it on? If you can not tolerate the planet it is on? Grade the ground first. If a man believes and expects great things of himself, it makes no odds where you put him, or what you show him, (of course, you cannot put him anywhere nor show him anything), he will be surrounded by grandeur. He's in the condition of a healthy & hungry man, who says to himself—How sweet this crust is!

If he despairs of himself, then Tophet[2] is his dwelling place, and he is in the condition of a sick man who is disgusted with the fruits of finest flavor.

Whether he sleeps or wakes, whether he runs or walks, whether he uses a microscope or a telescope, or his naked eye, a man never discovers anything, never overtakes anything or leaves anything behind, but himself. Whatever he says or does he merely reports himself. If he is in love, he *loves;* if he is in heaven he *enjoys,* if he is in hell he *suffers.* It is his condition that determines his locality.[3]

The principal, the only thing a man makes is his condition, or fate. Though commonly he does not know it, nor put up a sign to this effect, "My own destiny made & mended here" (not *yours*).[4] He is a master-workman in this business. He works 24 hours a day at it and gets it done. Whatever else he neglects or botches, no man was ever known to neglect this work. A great many pretend to make *shoes* chiefly, and would scout the idea that they make the hard times which they experience.

Each reaching and aspiration is an instinct with which all nature consists & cooperates, and therefore it is not in vain. But alas! each relaxing and desperation is an instinct too. To be active, well, happy, implies rare courage. To be ready to fight in a duel or a battle implies desperation, or that you hold your life cheap.

If you take this life to be simply what old religious folks pretend, (I mean the effete, gone to seed in a drought, mere human galls stung by the Devil once), then all your joy & serenity is reduced to grinning and bearing it. The fact is, you have got to take the world on your shoulders like Atlas[5] and put along with it. You will do this for an idea's sake, and your success will be in proportion to your devotion to ideas. It may make your back ache occasionally, but you will have the satisfaction of hanging it or twirling it to suit yourself. Cowards suffer, heroes enjoy. After a long day's walk with it, pitch it into a hollow place, sit down and eat your luncheon. Unexpectedly, by some immortal thoughts, you will be compensated. The bank whereon you sit will be a fragrant and flowery one, and your world in the hollow a sleek and light gazelle.[6]

Where is the "Unexplored land"[7] but in our own untried enterprises? To an adventurous spirit any place,—London, New York, Worcester, or his own yard, is "unexplored land," to seek which Freemont & Kane[8] travel so far. To a sluggish & defeated spirit even the Great Basin & the Polaris[9] are trivial places. If they ever get there (& indeed they are there now) they will want to sleep & give it up, just as they always do. These are the regions of the Known & of the Unknown. What is the use of going right over the old track again? There is an adder in the path[10] which your own feet have worn. You must make tracks into the Unknown. That is what you have your board & clothes for. Why do you ever mend your clothes, unless that, wearing them, you may mend your ways?

Let us sing.[11]

H.D.T.

ᨠ *Letter Forty-seven*

August 3, 1860, Friday; Concord, Massachusetts

The last recorded visit Blake had made to Concord was the one of the previous October, just before John Brown's raid at Harpers Ferry. At the time he wrote this letter Thoreau was enthusiastically, almost feverishly engaged in studying the woodlots of Concord and in fact had been so engaged for quite some time. His principal aim was to fill out more completely the first of his Darwinian treatises, "The Succession of Forest Trees," the main components of which also appear in his larger study, *The Dispersion of Seeds*. He spent a great deal of time in his attic study, where he worked on his manuscripts of these works, occasionally worked as well on his *Wild Fruits* and *The Fall of the Leaf* manuscripts, combed through his journals for material related to these projects, and read related books and articles. He and Channing left for Mount Monadnock on August 4 and returned on August 9.

Concord, August 3, 1860.

Mr. Blake,——

I some time ago asked Channing if he would not spend a week with me on Monadnoc; but he did not answer decidedly. Lately he has talked of an excursion somewhere, but I said that *now* I must wait till my sister returned from Plymouth, N.H. She has returned,——and accordingly, on receiving your note this morning, I made known its contents to Channing, in order to see how far I was engaged with him. The result is that he decides to go to Monadnoc to-morrow morning; so I must defer making an excursion with you and Brown to another season. Perhaps you will call as you pass the mountain. I send this by the earliest mail.

P.S.—That was a very insufficient visit you made here the last time. My mother is better, though far from well; and if you should chance along here any time after your journey, I trust that we shall all do better.

ᔋ Letter Forty-eight

November 4, 1860, Sunday; Concord, Massachusetts

Obviously, Blake and Brown had passed by Mount Monadnock, probably on a train, while Thoreau and Channing were on the mountain, but I have not been able to determine their destination. Thoreau at the time of his letter was still vigorously pursuing his various natural history studies, but by this time he had shifted his attention almost exclusively to *The Dispersion of Seeds*. Election Day fell two days after this letter was written. Abraham Lincoln received a majority vote among Northerners, but did not receive a majority of the popular vote. The combined opposition outpolled him by almost one million votes. He would be a minority president, lacking a clear mandate, and his inauguration would not take place until March. President James Buchanan was the "lame-duck" president during the intervening four months.

Concord Nov. 4 1860

Mr Blake,

I am glad to hear any particulars of your excursion. As for myself, I looked out for you somewhat on that Monday, when, it appears, you passed Monadnock—turned my glass upon several parties that were ascending the mountain half a mile on one side of us. In short, I came as near to seeing you as you to seeing me. I have no doubt that we should have had a good time if you had come, for I had, all ready, two good spruce houses,[1] in which you could stand up, complete in all respects, half a mile apart, and you & B[2] could have lodged by yourselves in one, if not with us.

We made an excellent beginning of our *mt.* life. You may remember that the Saturday previous was a stormy day. Well, we went up in the rain—wet through, and found ourselves in a cloud there at mid *pm.* in no situation to look about for the best place for a camp. So I proceeded at once, through the cloud, to that memorable stone "chunk yard,"[3] in which we made our humble camp once, and there, after putting our packs under a rock, having a good hatchet, I proceeded to build a substantial house, which C declared[4] the handsomest he ever saw. (He never camped out before, and was, no doubt, prejudiced in its favor.) This was done about dark, and by that time we were nearly as wet as if we had stood in a hogshead of water. We then built a fire before the door, directly on the site of our little camp of two years ago, and it took a long time to burn thro' its remains to the earth beneath. Standing before this, and turning round slowly, like meat that is roasting, we were as dry if not drier than ever after a few hours, & so, at last we "turned in."

This was a great deal better than going up there in fair weather, & having no adventure (not knowing how to appreciate either fair weather or foul) but dull common-place sleep in a useless house, & before a comparatively useless fire—such as we get every night. Of course, we thanked our stars,[5] when we saw them, which was about midnight, that they had seemingly withdrawn for a season. We had the *mt.* all to ourselves that *pm* & night. There was nobody going up that day to engrave his name on the summit, nor to gather blueberries.[6] The Genius[7] of the *mts.* saw us starting from Concord & it said,— There come two of our folks. Let us get ready for them— Get up a serious storm, that will send a-packing these holiday guests. (They may have their say another time.) Let us receive them with true *mt.* hospitality—kill the fatted cloud[8]— Let them know the value of a spruce roof, & of a fire of dead spruce stumps. Every bush dripped tears of joy at our advent. Fire did its best & received our thanks.— What could fire have done in fair weather?— Spruce roof got its share of our blessings. And then such a view of the wet rocks with the wet lichens on them, as we had the next morning, but did not get again!

We & the *mt.* had a sound season,[9] as the saying is. How glad we were to be wet in order that we might be dried!—how glad we were of the storm which made our house seem like a new home to us! This day's experience was indeed lucky for we did not have a thunder shower during all our stay. Perhaps our host reserved this attention in order to tempt us to come again.

Our next house was more substantial still. One side was rock, good for durability, the floor the same, & the roof which I made would have upheld a horse. I stood on it to do the shingling.

I noticed, when I was at the White *Mts.* last, several nuisances which render travelling there-abouts unpleasant. The chief of these was the *mt.* houses.[10] I might have supposed that the main attraction of that region even to citizens, lay in its wildness and unlikeness to the city, & yet they make it as much like the city as they can afford to. I heard that the Crawford House was lighted with gas, & had a large saloon, with its band of music, for dancing. But give me a spruce house made in the rain.

An old Concord farmer[11] tells me that he ascended Monadnock once, & danced on the top. How did that happen? Why, he being up there, a party of young men & women came up bringing boards & a fiddler, and having laid down the boards they made a level floor, on which they danced to the music of the fiddle. I suppose the tune was "Excelsior."[12] This reminds me of the fellow who climbed to the top of a very high spire, stood upright on the ball, & then hurrahed for—what? Why for Harrison & Tyler.[13] That's the kind of sound which most ambitious people emit when they culminate. They are wont to be singularly frivolous in the thin atmosphere; they can't contain themselves, though our comfort & their safety require it; it takes the pressure of many atmospheres to do this; & hence they helplessly evaporate there. It would seem, that, as they ascend, they breathe shorter and shorter, and at each *expiration,* some of their wits leave them, till, when they reach the pinnacle, they are so light headed as to be fit only to show how the wind sits. I suspect that Emerson's criticism called Monadnock[14] was inspired not by remembering the inhabitants of N. H. as they are in the valleys, so much as by meeting some of them on the *mt.* top.

After several nights' experience C came to the conclusion that he was "lying out doors," and inquired what was the largest beast that might nibble his legs there. I fear that he did not improve all the night, as he might have done, to sleep. I had asked him to go and spend a week there. We spent 5 nights, being gone 6 days, for C suggested that 6 working days made a week, & I saw that he was ready to *de-camp.* However, he found his account in it, as well as I.

We were seen to go up in the rain, grim & silent like 2 Genii of the storm,[15] by Fassett's men or boys,[16] but we were never identified afterward, though we were the subject of some conversation which we overheard. Five hundred persons at least came onto the *mt.* while we were there, but not one found our camp. We saw one party of three ladies & two gentlemen spread their blankets and spend the night on the top, & heard them converse, but they did not know that they had neighbors, who were comparatively old settlers. We spared them the chagrin which that knowledge would have caused them, & let them print their story in a newspaper[17] accordingly.

From what I heard of Fassett's infirmities[18] I concluded that his partner was Tap. He has moved about thirty rods further down the *mt.*, & is still hammering at a new castle there when you go by, while Tap is probably down cellar. Such is the Cerberus[19] that guards *this* passage. There always is one you know. This is not so bad to go by as the Glen House.[20] However, we left those Elysian fields[21] by a short cut of our own which departed just beyond where he is stationed.

Yes, to meet men on an honest and simple footing, meet with rebuffs, suffer from sore feet, as you did, aye & from a sore heart, as perhaps you also did,—all that is excellent. What a pity that that young prince[22] could not enjoy a little of the legitimate experience of travelling, be dealt with simply & truly though rudely. He might have been invited to some hospitable house in the country, had his bowl of bread & milk set before him, with a clean pin-a-fore,[23] been told that there were the punt[24] & the fishing rod, and he could amuse himself as he chose—might have swung a few birches,[25] dug out a wood-chuck, & had a regular good time, & finally been sent to bed with the boys,—and so never have been introduced to Mr. Everett at all. I have no doubt that this would have been a far more memorable & valuable experience than he got.

The snow-clad summit of *Mt.* Washington must have been a very interesting sight from Wachusett. How wholesome winter is seen far or near, how good above all mere sentimental warm-

blooded—short-lived, soft-hearted *moral* goodness, commonly
so called. Give me the goodness which has forgotten its own
deeds,—which God has seen to be good and let be. None of
your *just made perfect*—pickled eels![26] All that will save them will
be their picturesqueness, as with blasted trees. Whatever is and
is not ashamed to be is good. I value no moral goodness or
greatness unless it is good or great even as that snowy peak is.
Pray how could thirty feet of bowels[27] improve it? Nature is
goodness crystalized. You looked into the land of promise.[28]
Whatever beauty we behold, the more it is distant, serene, and
cold, the purer & more durable it is. It is better to warm ourselves with ice than with fire.

Tell Brown that he sent me more than the price of the book—
viz. a word from himself, for which I am greatly his debtor.

H. D. T.

☙ *Letter Forty-nine*

December 2, 1860, Sunday; Concord, Massachusetts

The results of the election earlier in the month reflected a deeply divided country. Lincoln's victory prompted secession conventions in seven states of the Deep South, and by the end of November the convention in South Carolina had rapidly moved toward a resolution to secede. Its Ordinance of Secession would not be formally issued, however, until December 20. On November 29 Thoreau had met with Alcott to discuss a meeting in Boston to commemorate the upcoming anniversary of the execution of John Brown. Alcott had a very bad cold at the time, apparently picked up four days before while attending a convention of the Massachusetts Teachers' Association, and he apparently passed the cold on to Thoreau, who began suffering the symptoms four days later, at about the time he wrote this letter to Blake. Rather than cancel his Waterbury lecture engagement so that he could convalesce, he kept the engagement (he delivered "Autumnal Tints") and exacerbated what he later described as an already severe cold. As planned, he stopped off at Worcester on December 11 and stayed the night with Blake. A friend of Blake's stopped by to meet Thoreau that evening and described him as a very sick man. If his cold did not worsen into bronchitis before the trip to Waterbury, it certainly did during or very soon afterward. He remained housebound throughout the winter, during which time he busied himself with his natural history manuscripts and reading. He would never recover.

Concord Dec 2d '60

Mr Blake,

I am going to Waterbury Ct. to lecture on the 11th inst. If you are to be at home, & it will be agreeable to you, I will spend the afternoon & night of the 10th with you & Brown.

H. D. Thoreau

↝ Letter Fifty

May 3, 1861, Friday; Concord, Massachusetts

The secession of South Carolina on December 20 had been followed by the secession of Mississippi (January 9), Florida (January 10), Alabama (January 11), Georgia (January 19), Louisiana (January 26), and Texas (February 1). These seven states formed a Confederate constitution later in February and named Jefferson Davis provisional president pending elections. The seceded states also occupied or insisted on the surrender of federal forts within their borders, but President Buchanan refused to surrender any forts. During this period of crisis Kansas was admitted to the Union (January 29). At the end of February Blake and Brown ice-skated and walked to Concord from Worcester, the trip taking two days, and spent a day and a half enjoying "a solid talk" with Thoreau, although he confessed that his "pipes were not in good order." Lincoln's inauguration took place on March 4. He announced that he had no plans to end slavery in those states where it already existed, but he also said he would not accept secession. Lincoln informed South Carolina in early April that he would resupply Fort Sumter in Charleston Harbor, and on April 10 Brigadier General Pierre Gustave Toutant Beauregard, in command of the provisional Confederate forces around the Union garrison, demanded its immediate surrender. When the garrison commander refused to surrender on April 12, Confederate batteries opened fire on the fort, which surrendered the following day. Lincoln issued a proclamation on April 15 announcing the existence of an "insurrection" and calling forth 75,000 of "the militia of the several States of the Union." Meanwhile, the physician attending Thoreau, Dr. Josiah Bartlett, the "Dr. B" mentioned near the end of the "Reading" chapter of *Walden*, had given his advice for Thoreau to visit warmer climes. Thoreau likely decided on Minnesota for a complex of reasons not mentioned in his letter. For one, a distant cousin had moved there a decade before with a respiratory ailment and had improved. Also, many stories were appearing in the Eastern press about the salutary effects of Minnesota's climate. The stories seem to have sprung from three facts: hundreds of thousands of Easterners suffered from tuberculosis, railroads to Minnesota (then relatively remote) were looking for more passengers, and pioneers in Minnesota were eager to encourage migration to their state. In any case, Thoreau stopped in Worcester on May 11 and spent two days with Blake and Brown. He was unable to walk because of his illness, so the three men instead toured the countryside in a horse-drawn carriage. Thoreau was on his way west, accompanied by the young naturalist Horace Mann Jr. (1844–1868), the son of the famous educator, whose family had recently moved to Concord. "Dunleith," just across the Mississippi River from Dubuque, Iowa, is now named East Dubuque, Illinois. Fulton, Illinois, also on the Mississippi River, is fifty miles south-southeast of East Dubuque. It is altogether fitting that the final word of this, Thoreau's last letter to Blake, is "moral."

Concord May 3d 1861

Mr Blake,

I am still as much an invalid as when you & Brown were here, if not more of one, and at this rate there is danger that the cold weather may come again, before I get over my bronchitis. The Doctor accordingly tells me that I must "clear out," to the West Indies, or elsewhere, he does not seem to care much where. But I decide against the West Indies, on account of their muggy heat in the summer, & the S. of Europe, on ac of the expense of time & money, and have at last concluded that it will be most expedient for me to try the air of Minnesota, say somewhere about St Paul. I am only waiting to be well enough to start—hope to get off within a week or 10 days.

The inland air may help me at once, or it may not. At any rate I am so much of an invalid that I shall have to study my

comfort in traveling to a remarkable degree—stopping to rest
&c &c if need be. I think to get a through ticket to Chicago—
with liberty to stop frequently on the way, making my first stop
of consequence at Niagara Falls—several days or a week, at a
private boarding house—then a night or day at Detroit—& as
much at Chicago, as my health may require.

At Chicago I can decide at what point (Fulton, Dunleith or
another) to strike the Mississippi & take a boat to St. Paul.

I trust to find a private boarding house in one or various
agreeable places in that region, & spend my time there.

I expect, and shall be prepared to be gone 3 months—& I
would like to return by a different route—perhaps Mackinaw
& Montreal.

I have thought of finding a companion, of course, yet not
seriously, because I had no right to offer myself as a companion to anybody—having such a peculiarly private & all absorbing but miserable business as *my* health, & not altogether *his*, to
attend to—causing me to stop here & go there &c &c unaccountably.

Nevertheless, I have just now decided to let you know of my
intentions, thinking it barely possible that you might like to
make a part or the whole of this journey, at the same time, &
that perhaps your own health may be such as to be benefitted
by it.

Pray let me know, if such a statement offers any temptations
to you. I write in great haste for the mail & must omit all the
moral.

H. D. Thoreau

Notes

Letter Two

1. The English had a reputation at the time for being particularly savvy in the ways of the world, in part because the technological marvels of the Industrial Revolution were concentrated there more than elsewhere. Another factor may have been the development in the British Isles during the late eighteenth and early nineteenth centuries of the common sense philosophy, although the movement was dominated by philosophers from Scotland rather than England.

2. William Shakespeare (1564–1616), *The Tempest* (1611), act 4, scene 1, lines 148–51, 154–55: "These our actors . . . were all spirits and / Are melted into air. . . . / And, like the baseless fabric of this vision . . . shall dissolve / And, like this insubstantial pageant faded, / Leave not a rack behind."

3. Matthew 20:22, "But Jesus answered and said, Ye know not what ye ask. Are ye able to drink of the cup that I shall drink of, and to be baptized with the baptism that I am baptized with? They say unto him, We are able."

4. 2 Kings 6:17, "And Elisha prayed, and said, Lord, I pray thee, open his eyes, that he may see. And the Lord opened the eyes of the young man; and he saw: and, behold, the mountain was full of horses and chariots of fire round about Elisha." Compare Revelations 2:7, 11, 17, 29; 3:6, 13, 22; "He that hath an ear, let him hear. . . ."

Letter Three

1. Genesis 3:19, "In the sweat of thy face shalt thou eat bread, till thou return unto the ground. . . ."
2. John 6:35, "And Jesus said unto them, I am the bread of life: he that cometh to me shall never hunger; and he that believeth on me shall never thirst."
3. Thoreau is likely alluding to *Dialogues Concerning Natural Religion* (London, 1779), by Scottish philosopher David Hume (1711–1776), which presents a discussion between fictional characters Cleanthes, who supports the Argument from Design (design in nature indicates the existence of God or an "Intelligent Designer"), and Philo, who points out that arguing from design in nature to an Intelligent Designer is a product of a defective imagination (flawed analogy and anthropocentric reasoning). Hume has Philo present several alternatives, none of which Cleanthes finds compelling, although one (Part 8) is strikingly similar to the evolutionary hypothesis of Charles Darwin (1809–1882).
4. A heavy mallet with a large wooden head.
5. An allusion to several New Testament passages about having "little faith," such as Matthew 8:26, "And he saith unto them, Why are ye fearful, O ye of little faith? Then he arose, and rebuked the winds and the sea; and there was a great calm."
6. An allusion to Isaiah 1:18, "Come now, and let us reason together, said the Lord: though your sins be as scarlet, they shall be as white as snow; though they be red like crimson, they shall be as wool."
7. Most of the great Western dramas (classical Greek, Renaissance, neoclassical) have five acts. In *Walden* Thoreau refers to "the play, it may be the tragedy, of life. . . ."
8. The Ten Commandments (Exodus 20, Deuteronomy 5) or any set of fundamental rules having authoritative weight. From the Greek *deka,* ten, and *logos,* word.
9. Parallax is the apparent displacement or difference of position of an object as seen from two different stations or points of view. Thoreau refers to a stellar parallax, which is the apparent dis-

placement of a fixed star as seen from the two extremes of the earth's orbit around the sun.

10. Thoreau may be quoting this phrase from Blake's letter by way of responding to Blake, but in any event this is likely an allusion to such biblical passages as Colossians 3:1, "If ye then be risen with Christ, seek those things which are above, where Christ sitteth on the right hand of God."

11. Thoreau may here be recalling the following remark in Emerson's lecture on "Goethe; or, The Writer," which was later (in 1850) published as one of the ten sections in *Representative Men:* "In [the writer's] eyes, a man is the faculty of reporting, and the universe is the possibility of being reported. In conversation, in calamity, he finds new materials; as our German poet [Goethe] said, 'Some god gave me the power to paint what I suffer.' He draws his rents from rage and pain."

12. Thoreau elaborates on this point in the "Solitude" chapter of *Walden:* "By a conscious effort of the mind we can stand aloof from actions and their consequences; and all things, good and bad, go by us like a torrent. We are not wholly involved in Nature. I may be either the drift-wood in the stream, or Indra in the sky looking down on it. I *may* be affected by a theatrical exhibition; on the other hand, I *may not* be affected by an actual event which appears to concern me much more. I only know myself as a human entity; the scene, so to speak, of thoughts and affections; and am sensible of a certain doubleness by which I can stand as remote from myself as from another. However intense my experience, I am conscious of the presence and criticism of a part of me, which, as it were, is not a part of me, but spectator, sharing no experience, but taking note of it; and that is no more I than it is you."

Letter Five

1. John 14:2, "In my Father's house are many mansions: if it were not so, I would have told you. I go to prepare a place for you." Thoreau probably did not intend the allusion, however.

2. This summary of Thoreau's economy is premised on his conception of what is most important in life—the soul, not the things of the body—and is a sort of précis of the heart of Jesus's Sermon on the Mount, Matthew 6:25–34, which begins and ends, "Therefore I say unto you, Take no thought for your life, what ye shall eat, or what ye shall drink; nor yet for your body, what ye shall put on. Is not the life more than meat, and the body than raiment? . . . Take therefore no thought for the morrow: for the morrow shall take thought for the things of itself. Sufficient unto the day is the evil thereof."

3. In classical mythology, King Minos of Crete built the labyrinth, a building of winding passages, to house the Minotaur, a half-human, half-bull creature that his wife Pasiphaë bore after having intercourse with a bull. (Minos had refused to sacrifice a bull to Poseidon, as the king had promised, so the god took revenge by causing his wife to desire the bull.) Minos required tribute from Athens in the form of young men and women to be sacrificed to the Minotaur. Theseus, an Athenian, volunteered to accompany one of these groups of victims into the labyrinth so that he could kill the Minotaur and stop the tributes. Ariadne, Minos's daughter, fell in love with Theseus and gave him thread to unwind as he wandered the labyrinth, a thread he was of course able to follow to safety after killing the Minotaur.

4. Thoreau's first book, *A Week on the Concord and Merrimack Rivers*, was officially published on May 30, 1849, although, as he mentions, he stopped by the Boston offices of his publisher, James Munroe and Company, on May 26 to pick up author's copies of the book and have some of those copies mailed to friends.

5. Theophilus "Theo" Brown (1811–1879), a tailor, was born in Rehoboth, Massachusetts, and in 1828 moved to Worcester, where he joined his brothers' tailoring firm. Their downtown shop became a gathering place for the intellectuals of the city. One such intellectual, Thomas Wentworth Higginson (1823–1911), described Brown as "a quite remarkable person . . . very original and agreeable, and rather the wit of the city." In 1868, six years after

Thoreau's death, Brown recalled Thoreau's manner of conversation as a "depth of earnestness and . . . [an] infinite depth of fun going on at the same time." In Letter 20 Thoreau tells Blake, "You will allow me to consider that I correspond with [Brown] through you," but by that time (December 1854) it is likely that Thoreau knew Blake summoned the Worcester intelligentsia to his house whenever one of Thoreau's longer letters arrived and read the letter or extracts from the letter to the assembly.

Letter Six

1. Thoreau's most frequent walking companion was the poet Ellery Channing, whose character was perhaps best summarized by the poet and author Emma Lazarus (1849–1887), who found him "a pathetic, impossible creature, whose cranks and oddities were submitted to on account of an innate nobility of character."
2. This and the quotation that follows in the letter are Thoreau's translations from the second volume of a two-volume set he checked out of the Harvard College Library on September 11, 1849, titled *Harivansa; ou, Histoire de la Famille de Hari . . .* (1834–35). "Harivansa" (sometimes "Harivamsa") is Sanskrit for "the lineage of Hari," or Krishna. The set Thoreau checked out contains a French translation from the original Sanskrit by Alexandre Langlois (1788–1854). The *Harivansa*, a poem of 16,374 verses, is widely regarded as part of the massive epic of ancient India, *Mahābhārata*, and "treats of the adventures of the family of Krishna, being divided into three parts: an introduction that traces the dynasty, the life and adventures of Krishna, and the conditions occurring during the kali yuga and the future condition of the world." Interestingly, Thoreau returned to this two-volume set in May 1851, when he was revising his early *Walden* manuscript, and extracted both of these passages into his journal, immediately after which he wrote, "Like some other preach-

ers, I have added my texts, derived from the Chinese and Hindoo scriptures, long after my discourse [that is, the version of *Walden* he was working on at that time] was written." Either in the fall of 1849 or in the early summer of 1851 he translated a portion of the *Harivansa* on "The Transmigration of the Seven Brahmans." In his journal entry of June 29, 1851, he wrote, "It is unavoidable, the idea of transmigration; not merely a fancy of the poets, but an instinct of the race."

3. See the preceding note.

4. Throughout the first half of 1849 Russia had gradually become involved in the insurrections that were taking place in Hungary and Transylvania, actually joining Austrian forces in a June 1849 invasion of those countries. When the insurrectionists were defeated in August, many of the leaders sought refuge in Turkey, and when the conquerors exercised existing treaties to apply for the extradition of those leaders, Turkey broke off diplomatic relations. The French and the British supported the Turks by sending naval vessels to the eastern Mediterranean. A full-scale European war seemed inevitable but was temporarily averted. This deployment of naval forces by Britain's foreign secretary, Lord Palmerston (Henry John Temple, 1784–1865), whose abrasive style earned him the nickname "Lord Pumice Stone," prompted the British press to coin the phrase "gunboat diplomacy."

5. During the Revolutionary War newspapers in the United States cost about six cents, but the development of the steam printing press dramatically cut printing costs and sped up production, which inaugurated the first mass-circulation newspapers. The first penny newspapers, Horatio David Sheppard's *New-York Morning Post* and Benjamin H. Day's *New York Sun,* began publication in 1833.

6. In *Le Chapon et la Poularde* (1763), the French author and philosopher Voltaire (1694–1778) wrote, "They only use speech to disguise their thoughts." French statesman Charles-Maurice de Talleyrand (1754–1838) is usually credited with the sentence

"Speech was given to man to disguise his thoughts or to help him hide his thoughts," but Captain Rees Howell Gronow (1794–1865), in his *Recollections and Anecdotes* (1862), asserts that the words were those of Philippe-François-Casimir, Count of Montrond (1769–1843), a French wit and poet. Thoreau is known to have read British poet Oliver Goldsmith (1728–1774), who in *The Bee* (1759) expressed the same general idea: "The true use of speech is not so much to express our wants as to conceal them."

Letter Seven

1. The phrase Native Americans used to express their idea of God. In his extremely wide reading in early histories of Native Americans, Thoreau came across the phrase often. In 1849, for instance, he read and extracted into his reading notes a source that spoke of a "proverbial tradition" of the Oneida Indians that "the Great Spirit gave the white man a plough, and the red man a bow and arrow, and sent them into the world by different paths, each to get his living in his own way."

2. This is the earliest extant instance of Thoreau's use of this phrase, which later he mentions regularly in his journal, although he very likely used the phrase in earlier entries that he cut out of his bound journal volumes in preparing lectures. The last section of his essay "Wild Apples" is titled "The 'Frozen-Thawed' Apple," and he thus describes them there: "Let the frost come to freeze [the wild apples] first solid as stones, and then the rain or a warm winter day, to thaw them, and they will seem to have borrowed a flavor from heaven through the medium of the air in which they hang. . . . Now [my companion and I] both greedily fill our pockets with them—bending to drink the cup and save our lappets from the overflowing juice—and grow more social with their wine."

3. Thoreau may be alluding here to Luke 6:39, "And he spake a parable unto them, Can the blind lead the blind? shall they not

both fall into the ditch?" He also appears to be using the "understanding" component of the famous distinction Samuel Taylor Coleridge (1772–1834) made between "Reason" and "Understanding." Generally, the understanding deals with facts whereas the reason deals with truths, as Thoreau suggests in an early journal entry, where he wrote, "The fact will one day flower out into a truth. The reason will mature and fructify what the understanding had cultivated."

4. Possibly an allusion to part 1, stage 5, of *The Pilgrim's Progress from This World to that which Is to Come, Delivered under the Similitude of a Dream* by John Bunyan (1628–1688), wherein Christian and his companions, Pliable and Obstinate, encountered "a very miry slough, that was in the midst of the plain; and they, being heedless, did both fall suddenly into the bog. The name of the slough was Despond. Here, therefore, they wallowed for a time, being grievously bedaubed with the dirt; and Christian, because of the burden that was on his back, began to sink in the mire."

5. Honoré de Balzac (1799–1850), the French novelist, used this phrase in the last paragraph of his short story "The Fair Imperia Married," which first appeared in his *Contes Drolatiques* (*Droll Stories*; Paris, 1832): "Phist! Here she is astride a sunbeam with a volume that is ready to burst with merry meteors!"

6. Unlike Romans of the early Christian era, who preferred cremation after death, early Christians preferred burial, which required land and was therefore extremely expensive. A few wealthy Christian landowners within a three-mile radius of Rome allowed their land to be used as burial sites, and these sites became the catacombs. From the first through the fifth century, Christians dug an estimated four hundred miles of tomb-lined tunnels with networks of galleries upwards of five layers deep in order to maximize the donated land, as well as to be near martyrs and saints already buried there. When invading barbarians began ransacking the catacombs in the 800s, the remains were removed to the safety of inner-city churches, and the catacombs were filled in. For the next one thousand years the catacombs were more or less

forgotten, but increasingly during the 1840s and 1850s they were excavated and became tourist attractions.

7. A phrase taken from the title of Shakespeare's comedy, written in or shortly after 1598.

8. In 1812 the Grimm Brothers, Jacob (1785–1863) and Wilhelm (1786–1859), published *Kinder- und Hausmärchen* (*Children and Household Tales*), an unpretentious book containing eighty-six numbered folktales, one of which was "Der Froschkönig; oder, Der eiserne Heinrich" ("The Frog King; or, Iron Henry"), a tale featuring a handsome prince disguised as an ugly frog who retrieved a princess's golden ball from a pond in exchange for her vow to "love me and accept me as a companion and playmate, and let me sit next to you at your table and eat from your golden plate and drink from your cup and sleep in your bed."

9. The best age—such as the golden age of innocence or the golden age of literature. Hesiod defines the golden age as the patriarchal period of the Titan god Saturn.

10. In Greek mythology, the home of the gods.

11. Apparently an imagined hypothesis, very likely based on the Hindu doctrine of the transmigration of the soul.

12. Thoreau's first book, *A Week on the Concord and Merrimack Rivers*, contains a long section on "Friendship" in the "Wednesday" chapter.

13. This is an extremely important concept for Thoreau. In the "Friendship" section of his first book, he writes, "True Friendship can afford true knowledge. . . . If I can see my Friend's virtues more distinctly than another's, his faults too are made more conspicuous by contrast. . . . I have never known one who could bear criticism, who could not be flattered, who would not bribe his judge, or was content that the truth should be loved always better than himself." As mentioned earlier, Thoreau's falling-out with his friend Emerson in 1849 was occasioned largely by Emerson's failure to critique the very book in which those words were published—until after the book was published.

Letter Eight

1. Thoreau is pointing to the original sense of the word, "scurfy," or covered with little dry scales of skin.

2. This is an extremely important concept for Thoreau, one that he fleshes out most interestingly near the end of his essay "Autumnal Tints," where he writes, "Why, it takes a sharp shooter to bring down even such trivial game as snipes and woodcocks; he must take very particular aim, and know what he is aiming at. He would stand a very small chance, if he fired at random into the sky, being told that snipes were flying there. And so is it with him that shoots at beauty; though he wait till the sky falls, he will not bag any, if he does not already know its seasons and haunts, and the color of its wing,—if he has not dreamed of it, so that he can *anticipate* it; then, indeed, he flushes it at every step, shoots double and on the wing, with both barrels, even in cornfields. The sportsman trains himself, dresses and watches unweariedly, and loads and primes for his particular game. He prays for it, and offers sacrifices, and so he gets it. After due and long preparation, schooling his eye and hand, dreaming awake and asleep, with gun and paddle and boat he goes out after meadow-hens, which most of his townsmen never saw nor dreamed of, and paddles for miles against a head-wind, and wades in water up to his knees, being out all day without his dinner, and *therefore* he gets them. He had them half-way into his bag when he started, and has only to shove them down. The true sportsman can shoot you almost any of his game from his windows: what else has he windows or eyes for? It comes and perches at last on the barrel of his gun; but the rest of the world never see it *with the feathers on.* The geese fly exactly under his zenith, and honk when they get there, and he will keep himself supplied by firing up his chimney; twenty musquash have the refusal of each one of his traps before it is empty. If he lives, and his game-spirit increases, heaven and earth shall fail him sooner than game; and when he dies, he will go to more extensive, and, perchance, happier hunting-grounds.

The fisherman, too, dreams of fish, sees a bobbing cork in his dreams, till he can almost catch them in his sink-spout."

3. The early Greek philosopher Pythagoras was the first to suggest the notion so beautifully expressed by Shakespeare in *The Merchant of Venice* (1596–97; act 5, scene 1, lines 60–62): "There's not the smallest orb which thou beholdst / But in his motion like an angel sings, / Still quiring to the young-eyed cherubims." The notion is generally known as "the music of the spheres."

4. Thoreau mentions in his journal entry of June 8, 1850, that "[w]hen the frogs dream . . . then is summer begun." He uses *dream* here in the obsolete sense of "to make music or melody, to play on an instrument, rejoice."

5. Thoreau may here be thinking in part of his own bean field at Walden Pond, which he describes in his early manuscript as being an "upland" field where life everlasting (cudweed, or *Gnaphalium obtusifolium*) grew before the spring of 1845, when he began clearing it for cultivation.

6. During the fall and early winter of 1849 Thoreau composed three lectures that he titled "An Excursion to Cape Cod." However, at about the time he completed his work on these lectures he was asked to deliver *two* lectures before his hometown lyceum, so he revised them to accommodate the request, delivering them a week apart in late January 1850. Emerson reported that the audience "laughed till they cried, when it was read to them." Amusingly, just a week later Thoreau was asked to roll those two into a single lecture for delivery at a lyceum in South Danvers, Massachusetts, on February 18, 1850, a delivery that met with "a decided acceptance." Although this single "Cape Cod" lecture would appear to be the one Thoreau speaks of, it is odd that he characterizes it as "no better calculated for a promiscuous audience than the last two" he had read, for which see the following note. There is no record of Thoreau having delivered the "Cape Cod" lecture in Worcester.

7. Interestingly, Thoreau delivered his three "Walden" lectures in Worcester one week apart in late May and early June 1849. The

last two of those three lectures, however, were far more philosophically oriented than the first one, which was about economic matters that Yankees could more easily get their minds around. In general, the three lectures correspond to the *Walden* chapters "Economy" (first lecture), "Where I Lived, and What I Lived For" (second lecture), and a sort of amalgam of the next five chapters: "Reading," "Sounds," "Solitude," "Visitors," and "The Bean-Field." A journalist who had not heard the first lecture in Worcester expressed regret at missing it because "the commendations we hear of it assure us that it would have been a source of enjoyment to us." This journalist did hear the second lecture the following week, but he stated that he was disappointed, primarily because he found Thoreau imitative in both manner and content: "[T]he lecture was a better imitation of Emerson than we should have thought possible. . . ." The only thing like a review of the third "Walden" lecture was "the incandescent gibberish of [a] letter from a self-described member of Worcester's 'sofa lolling literati,'" as Ronald Wesley Hoag has described it. The beginning of the letter is indicative of its general tenor and suggests that Thoreau had some reason to be concerned about delivering another lecture in Worcester, even one so well suited to popular taste as "An Excursion to Cape Cod" seems to have been: "Henry D. Thoreau of Concord had better go home and ask his mother if she 'knows he's out.' Doubtless she, (Nature) will say she missed him who is the soul of Walden. Be satisfied, Thoreau, to be the soul of Waldenwood. To be frank with you, you are better as a woodman, or say, a woodpecker, than as a cockney philosopher, or a city parrot, to mimick the voices of canaries or cat owls, of Emersons, or Carlyles—or I beseech you if you must sing in cities, to warble *only* your 'native wood notes wild.'"

8. A fountain in Pieria, sacred to the Muses and supposedly conferring inspiration or learning on anyone who drank from it, and probably most famously mentioned in English by the British poet Alexander Pope (1688–1744), who wrote in his "Essay on

Criticism," "A little learning is a dangerous thing; / Drink deep, or taste not the Pierian spring. . . ."

9. In part 2, stage 25, of Bunyan's *The Pilgrim's Progress*, the weary pilgrims Christian and Hopeful enter "the land of Beulah, where the sun shines night and day," seeking rest. Although this country "was common for pilgrims," it was highly unaccommodating because "the bells did so ring, and the trumpets continually sound so melodiously, that they could not sleep. . . ." The other pilgrims who were there also so persistently sang the praises of the land that Christian and Hopeful could not rest at all. This land-of-Beulah section ends with the sentence from which Thoreau borrows: "In this land [Christian and Hopeful] heard nothing, saw nothing, felt nothing, smelt nothing, tasted nothing, that was offensive to their stomach or mind; only when they tasted of the water of the river over which they were to go, they thought that tasted a little bitterish to the palate, but it proved sweeter when 'twas down."

Letter Nine

1. This sentence is an important gloss on Thoreau's famous clause from his essay "Walking," which he was working on at this time: "[I]n Wildness is the preservation of the world."

2. An allusion to the Great Dismal Swamp, which consists of more than 100,000 acres of wilderness and largely inaccessible swampy forest land in North Carolina and Virginia. In the "Sounds" chapter of *Walden* Thoreau uses the same image in connection with the "bright saloons" of railroad cars to represent the opposite extreme of civilization: "Far through unfrequented woods on the confines of towns, where once only the hunter penetrated by day, in the darkest night dart these bright saloons without the knowledge of their inhabitants; this moment stopping at some brilliant stationhouse in town or city, where a social crowd is gathered, the next in the Dismal Swamp, scaring the owl and fox."

3. Thoreau is certainly recalling here his September 1846 climb up

a ridge on the side of Mount Katahdin in Maine, which he describes in his posthumously published book, *The Maine Woods:* "Leaving [the mountain stream or "torrent"] at last, I began to work my way, scarcely less arduous than Satan's anciently through Chaos, up the nearest, though not the highest peak. At first scrambling on all fours over the tops of ancient black spruce-trees (*Abies nigra*), old as the flood, from two to ten or twelve feet in height, their tops flat and spreading, and their foliage blue, and nipt with cold, as if for centuries they had ceased growing upward against the bleak sky, the solid cold. I walked some good rods erect upon the tops of these trees, which were overgrown with moss and mountain-cranberries. It seemed that in the course of time they had filled up the intervals between the huge rocks, and the cold wind had uniformly levelled all over. Here the principle of vegetation was hard put to it. There was apparently a belt of this kind running quite round the mountain, though, perhaps, nowhere so remarkable as here. Once, slumping through, I looked down ten feet, into a dark and cavernous region, and saw the stem of a spruce, on whose top I stood, as on a mass of coarse basket-work, fully nine inches in diameter at the ground. These holes were bears' dens, and the bears were even then at home. This was the sort of garden I made my way *over*, for an eighth of a mile, at the risk, it is true, of treading on some of the plants, not seeing any path *through* it,—certainly the most treacherous and porous country I ever travelled."

4. Matthew 6.3, "But when thou doest alms, let not thy left hand know what thy right hand doeth."

5. The images here unmistakably point to one he used in the penultimate paragraph of the second chapter of *Walden:* "If you stand right fronting and face to face to a fact, you will see the sun glimmer on both its surfaces, as if it were a cimeter, and feel its sweet edge dividing you through the heart and marrow, and so you will happily conclude your mortal career. Be it life or death, we crave only reality."

Letter Ten

1. In his journal entry of July 2, 1852, Thoreau noted, "This is my year of observation, & I fancy that my friends are also more devoted to outward observation than ever before—as if it were an epidemic." The seasonal or phenological lists and charts he later compiled from his journal are in fact most comprehensive for the year 1852.

2. Tin or other reflective materials were tied to scarecrows to attract the attention of, and therefore help to scare off, crows.

3. The second highest hill in Worcester County, located in the town of Paxton, six miles northwest of downtown Worcester, Massachusetts.

4. A temple without a roof is called a hypaethral temple, such a one as Thoreau likens in his posthumously published essay "Life without Principle" to the mind: "Shall the mind be a public arena, where the affairs of the street and the gossip of the tea-table chiefly are discussed? Or shall it be a quarter of heaven itself—an hypaethral temple, consecrated to the service of the gods?"

5. A town ten miles northwest of downtown Worcester, Massachusetts, just north of the town of Paxton.

6. Thoreau mentions near the end of Letter 16 that he had read this fact, but I have not been able to locate his source.

7. The Free-Soil Party was an influential third party in the United States from 1848 to 1854. Its main objective was to prevent the extension of slavery into the new territories acquired from Mexico. The party evolved from antislavery and otherwise discontented elements in the two major political parties of the time, the Democrats and the Whigs. It was eclipsed in 1854 by the Republican Party, which incorporated Free-Soil goals.

8. A large merchant ship in the British trade with India. Thoreau's subsequent images recall the classic adventure story *Robinson Crusoe* by Daniel Defoe (1660–1731), published in 1719 and based

on the marooning of Scotsman Alexander Selkirk (1676–1721) from 1703 to 1709 on the island of Juan Fernández, four hundred miles off the coast of Chile.

9. Many legal documents are required to be written in indelible ink. The earliest instance of this requirement I have been able to locate was for European health permits issued to travelers during the sixteenth century, which also had to have seals affixed from the issuing authorities.

Letter Eleven, Enclosure 1

1. From Aeolus, the Greek god of the wind, an aeolian harp is a small box across which strings of different thicknesses are stretched, the strings tuned to resonate in unison with one another. These devices, which were extremely popular during the Romantic era, are set in open windows so that wind blowing across the strings creates rising and falling harmonies. Coleridge wrote a well-known poem titled "The Aeolian Harp"; and in his famous essay "A Defence of Poetry," Percy Bysshe Shelley (1792–1822) wrote, "Man is an instrument over which a series of external and internal impressions are driven, like the alternations of an ever-changing wind over an aeolian lyre, which move it by their motion to ever-changing melody."

2. Thoreau's own verses.

3. I have not been able to locate Thoreau's source for this phrase.

4. Baron Frederick von der Trenck (1745–1794) relates in his autobiography, *The Life of Baron Frederick Trenck* (1792), that after ten years' imprisonment in the Fortress of Magdeburg in Germany, he had tunneled to within six or seven feet of escape when sentinels heard him as he "went backward and forward to bring [his] earth bags" out of the tunnel. When the sentinels and several others searched his cell unsuccessfully the next day, one of the party "said to the sentinel, 'Blockhead! you have heard some mole underground, and not Trenck. How, indeed, could it be,

that he should work underground, at such a distance from his dungeon?'"

5. Thoreau's own poem. I emend the source by removing the apostrophe from "Can'st" at the beginning of the second stanza.

6. Thoreau's own poem.

7. An archaic word for a churl or villain, although the word is used in Scotland to denote a sturdy fellow.

Letter Eleven, Enclosure 2

1. Officially called the United Society of Believers in Christ's Second Appearing or the Millennial Church, Shakers are an American celibate and communistic sect founded by Ann Lee (1736–1784), the daughter of a blacksmith from Manchester, England. Initially she belonged to a "Shaking Quaker" offshoot of the English Quakers, and was frequently imprisoned for breaking the Sabbath by dancing and shouting, and for blasphemy. She reported that on one occasion, while being examined by four clergymen of the established church, she spoke to them for four hours in seventy-two tongues. While in prison she claimed to have had a revelation that a complete renunciation of sex, or "the lust of generation," added to a full and explicit confession before witnesses of all the sins committed under its influence, was the only possible means of salvation. After this, probably in 1770, she was chosen by the society as Mother in spiritual matters and called herself "Ann, the Word." In 1774 a revelation bade her take a select band to America. She and her followers resided for two years in New York City before purchasing a tract of land at Niskayuna, in the township of Watervliet, just north of Albany.

2. Amusingly, Emerson changed this word in his edition of this enclosure to "marriage," which makes nonsense of the sentence, as Walter Harding points out in *The New Thoreau Handbook* (New York, 1980). On the basis of Harding's observation, I restore Thoreau's word.

3. In his essay "Friendship," published in 1841, Emerson asserts, "Almost all people descend to meet. All association must be a compromise, and, what is worst, the very flower and aroma of the flower of each of the beautiful natures disappears as they approach each other." Thoreau used the phrase later in his "A Plea for Captain John Brown" without quotation marks: "I do not believe in lawyers, in that mode of attacking or defending a man, because you descend to meet the judge on his own ground, and, in cases of the highest importance, it is of no consequence whether a man breaks a human law or not."

4. Isacus J. Biberg, "Oeconomica Naturæ, quam Præside Dn. D. Carolo Linnæo . . ." (Upsala, Sweden; March 4, 1749), in Caroli Linnæi (1707–1778), *Amœnitates Academicæ; seu Dissertationes Variæ, Physicæ, Medicæ, Botanicæ* . . . (Holmiæ: Apud Laurentium Savium, 1751), vol. 2. Thoreau checked this volume out of the Harvard College Library on May 24, 1852, and extracted the original Latin version of this passage into his reading notebook on natural history, which he called his "Fact Book" and, later, "Commonplace Book."

5. Swedish botanist Carl Linnaeus first published his sexual system of botanical classification in *Systema Naturae* (1735) and applied it to every then-known species in *Species Plantarum* (1753). Thoreau appears not to have read either of these works, so he probably read about the Linnaean system in either Richard Pulteney's *A General View of the Writings of Linnaeus* . . . (2d ed., 1805) or Dietrich Johann Heinrich Stöver's *The Life of Sir Charles Linnaeus* . . . (London, 1794), both of which sources Thoreau read in the winter of 1851–52.

6. Matthew 7:19–20, "Every tree that bringeth not forth good fruit is hewn down, and cast into the fire. Wherefore by their fruits ye shall know them."

Letter Twelve

1. Thoreau surveyed John B. Moore's 205-acre farm on February 10–12 and 18–19, 1853, and he likely spent as many hours at

his desk preparing the survey as he spent in the field gathering the data. Moore's farm straddled the eastern end of Revolutionary Ridge in Concord, and was subdivided and sold off in 1860.

2. During the seventy-six days from December 13, 1852, to February 27, 1853, Thoreau surveyed twice for Daniel Weston and once for Virgil Fuller, Henry L. Shattuck, Humphrey Hunt, Elijah Davis, John Le Grosse, Turner Bryant, James Wood, and John B. Moore—spending a total of at least sixteen days in the field, not to mention the time he spent at his desk assembling his field data and preparing his surveys.

3. The only lecture Thoreau delivered during the 1852–53 season was his "Excursion to Moosehead Lake," which he read before his fellow townspeople on December 14, 1853. He was not paid for any of his hometown lectures, and he dearly needed income to settle the substantial debt he had incurred for underwriting the publication of *A Week*.

4. The Latin word *anima* means breath, air, and soul. In English anima means life principle or soul. Thoreau's sense, then, is the soul force that makes possible the movement of otherwise inert matter.

5. The phrase "Manifest Destiny" was first used by the American journalist and diplomat John Louis O'Sullivan (1813–1895) in an editorial supporting the annexation of Texas, the editorial appearing in the July-August 1845 edition of the *United States Magazine and Democratic Review*. The phrase was later used by expansionists in all political parties to justify the acquisition of California and the Oregon Territory.

6. Miguel de Cervantes (1547–1616) in *Don Quixote de la Mancha* (1605) has his famous character several times describe himself as a "captive knight."

7. Manifest Destiny postulates a westward movement of civilization, the last terrestrial stage of which would be crossing the Pacific Ocean. Thoreau uses Japan here to mark the westernmost terminus of Manifest Destiny's circumnavigation of the globe.

8. Thoreau in June 1850 had read of the history of Assyria in

Nineveh and Its Remains; with an Account of a Visit to the Chaldean Christians of Kurdistan, and the Yezidis, or Devil-Worshippers; and an Inquiry into the Manner of Arts of the Ancient Assyrians by Sir Austen Henry Layard (1817–1894), who describes ancient bas-reliefs of sheep and goats.

9. The major contenders for the presidency in the election of 1852 were the Whig candidate Winfield Scott (1786–1866) and the Democratic candidate Franklin Pierce (1804–1869), the latter of whom was elected the fourteenth president.

10. Paul counsels in Galatians 6:9, "And let us not grow weary of doing good; for in due season we shall reap a blessing, if we faint not." Do-goodism was alive and well in antebellum America.

11. Thoreau observed this phenomenon while living at Walden Pond and stated in the "House-Warming" chapter of *Walden*, "I inferred that the infinite number of minute bubbles which I had first seen against the under surface of the ice were now frozen in . . . and that each, in its degree, had operated like a burning glass on the ice beneath to melt and rot it." He also noted that these "little air-guns . . . contribute to make the ice crack and whoop."

12. Matthew 19:24, "And again I say unto you, It is easier for a camel to go through the eye of a needle, than for a rich man to enter into the kingdom of God."

13. A reference to the parable of the talents, Matthew 25:14–30, wherein each of three servants are given five talents, two talents, and one talent, respectively. (A talent here is a unit of money.) The servants who received two and five talents invested and eventually doubled their money, but the servant who received the single talent buried his money to keep it safe. Because he squandered his talent, he was cast "into outer darkness. . . ."

14. Loammi Baldwin (1744–1807), an American engineer and a colonel in the Revolutionary War who commanded the Woburn Militia at the Battle of Lexington and Concord, discovered the apple which became known as the Baldwin apple in Wilmington, Massachusetts, fourteen miles northwest of Boston, while he was surveying the route of the Middlesex Canal in 1784. The

eleventh of the twelve labors Hercules had to perform for Eurystheus was to get for him the golden apples which Hera had given to Zeus as a wedding gift and which Zeus kept in the garden of the Hesperides, the daughters of Atlas. Hercules had to take the world off Atlas's shoulders so that the Titan could get the apples. Hercules tricked Atlas into taking the world back, but Eurystheus was not allowed to keep the golden apples, which the goddess Athena returned to the garden of the Hesperides.

15. The manuscript actually reads "Good," but Thoreau's intention here is clear, particularly since this word is followed by "who."

16. In the friendship section of the "Wednesday" chapter of his first book, *A Week on the Concord and Merrimack Rivers*, Thoreau writes, "The true and not despairing Friend will address his Friend in some such terms as these: 'I never asked thy leave to let me love thee,—I have a right. I love thee not as something private and personal, which is *your own*, but as something universal and worthy of love, *which I have found*. O, how I think of you! You are purely good,—you are infinitely good. I can trust you forever. I did not think that humanity was so rich. Give me an opportunity to live.'"

17. In part I, stage 8, of Bunyan's *The Pilgrim's Progress*, the pilgrims Christian and Hopeful ascended the Delectable Mountains and were taken by the shepherds Knowledge, Experience, Watchful, and Sincere to a place in a bottom that was "a by-way to hell, a way that hypocrites go in at," as well as to the tops of three of the mountains, Error, Caution, and Clear.

18. Thoreau appears here to be stretching for a linguistic pun based on the etymological root *unus*, Latin for "one," and the suffix *-ion*, indicating a substantive of condition or action.

19. As mentioned in the footnote, Thoreau's "An Excursion to Canada," the account of his journey to that country with Ellery Channing in the fall of 1850, had appeared in the first three issues (January–March 1853) of the new *Putnam's Magazine*; but a dispute with Curtis, the editor, caused the serialization to be halted abruptly. The entire narrative was not published until

after Thoreau's death, when it appeared as *A Yankee in Canada* (Boston, 1866). Many readers find it the least inspired of Thoreau's excursions, and Thoreau himself inauspiciously begins the book with the observation that what he got by going to Canada was a cold!

20. The wealth pouring into the U.S. Treasury from California gold had been impressive in the years after the gold rush that began in 1849.

21. Mark 8:36, "For what shall it profit a man, if he gain the whole world, and lose his own soul?" Well-known nature writer Joseph Wood Krutch (1893–1970) rightly asserted that Thoreau spent his entire life preaching from this text; in fact, within four months after *Walden* was published he wrote a lecture titled "What Shall It Profit" which began and ended with this scripture. He first delivered this lecture in Providence, Rhode Island, on December 6, 1854; a revised version of it was posthumously published in the *Atlantic Monthly* as "Life without Principle."

Letter Thirteen

1. Thoreau points out in his book *Cape Cod* that the "sun-squawl or sun-fish"—a large jellyfish—is "one of the lowest forms of animal life," a bit of information he may have picked up from James Eliot Cabot (1821–1903) or Pierre Jean Éduard Desor (1811–1882) on August 1, 1851, when he discussed with the two naturalists in Boston an unusual specimen (then named *Oceania tubulosa,* but now *Oceania armata*) which he had found on the beach during an excursion he had just completed to Plymouth, Massachusetts.

2. Thoreau here appears to interpret the expression "dog chasing its tail" as indicating that the dog fails to realize that the tail is part of its body, although the kettle complicates the matter.

3. In the "Dandelion" section of his book-length manuscript *Wild Fruits,* not published until 2000, Thoreau states, "If [boys] can

blow off all the seeds at one puff, then their mothers do not want them." Early in the twentieth century Alice Johnson Jones (b. 1848) offered a different version of the story: "When three puffs of breath failed to blow all the tufted seeds from a dandelion globe, the shout arose, 'Your mother wants you!'"

4. Thoreau appears here to be referring to the dandelion seed—or perhaps to what he had "read of something happening to another the other day."

5. An expression taught to children learning arithmetic to help them remember to "carry one" into the next column when they add a column of numbers totaling ten or more. In England the phrase is a slang expression meaning "limp" or "miss a beat."

6. From the poem "To the Lady Margaret, Countess of Cumberland," by British poet Samuel Daniel (1562–1619). Thoreau used this couplet in his 1859 essay "A Plea for Captain John Brown."

7. "The Devil and Tom Walker" was "a popular saying, prevalent throughout New England," according to Washington Irving (1783–1859), who published a short story of that title in 1800. In Irving's telling, Tom Walker struck a Faustian bargain with the devil, turned usurer in Boston, made a fortune loaning money to poor folks at exorbitant rates, and had his own loan come due when he impatiently responded to a poor land-jobber's assertion that he had made so much money out of the jobber, "The devil take me if I have made a farthing!" At that moment a black man on a black horse knocked at the office door, Tom went to open it, and was never seen again. The good people of Boston searched his office, but all his coffers were found empty; and during the night his house caught fire and was burned to the ground.

8. This phrase echoes the ending of *Walden*, which was published sixteen months after this letter was written: "The light which puts out our eyes is darkness to us. Only that day dawns to which we are awake. There is more day to dawn. The sun is but a morning star."

9. Thoreau's cousin Charles Howard Dunbar (b. 1808) lived in

Haverhill, Massachusetts, twenty-eight miles north of Boston, near the New Hampshire border. In the spring of 1850 he arranged for Thoreau to survey the estate of Nehemiah Emerson (1749–1832) for the heirs. Apparently Blake visited Thoreau in Haverhill on that occasion, although this is the only record of such a visit. Probably Dunbar was also instrumental in arranging this surveying job for Thoreau, who spent seventeen days surveying for three landowners in Haverhill later in the month.

10. Thoreau writes in the final chapter of *Walden*, "I desire to speak somewhere *without* bounds; like a man in a waking moment, to men in their waking moments; for I am convinced that I cannot exaggerate enough even to lay the foundation of a true expression."

11. Homer (ca. eighth century B.C.) in the *Odyssey*, book 11, says that the Titans "were fain to pile Ossa on Olympus, and Pelion, with its waving forests, on Ossa, so that heaven might be scaled." Pelion and Ossa are two mountains in Greece. The expression "heaping Pelion upon Ossa" means adding difficulty to difficulty.

12. A carriage pulled by four horses.

Letter Fourteen

1. As mentioned in the headnote to this letter, Thoreau lectured before his hometown lyceum on December 14. He had surveyed the previous month for the heirs of John Richardson, had surveyed earlier this month for George Brooks, and when he wrote this letter was in the midst of surveying for James P. Brown.

2. In his journal entry of June 3, 1851, Thoreau mentions having spoken the previous day in Boston with Captain John Downes (1786–1855), the commandant of the Naval Yard in Boston, who had once seen "the common sucker in numbers piling up stones as big as his fist (like the piles which I have seen) taking them up or moving them with their mouths." In the "Saturday" chapter of *A Week*, Thoreau had attributed "the curious circular

nests" to "the Lamprey Eel, *Petromyzon Americanus*, the American Stone-Sucker," the nests being "as large as a cart-wheel, a foot or two in height, and sometimes rising half a foot above the surface of the water. They collect these stones, of the size of a hen's egg, with their mouths, as their name implies, and are said to fashion them into circles with their tails." Actually, these nests are built and defended by the male fallfish (*Semotilus corporalis*).

3. Thoreau wrote in his journal for December 3, "I see that muskrats have not only erected cabins, but since the river rose have in some places dug galleries a rod into the bank pushing the sand behind them into the water— So they dig these now as places of retreat merely or for the same purpose as the cabins apparently— One I explored this afternoon was formed in a low shore (Hubbard's Bathing Place) at a spot where there were no weeds to make a cabin of—and was apparently never completed, perhaps because the shore was too low."

4. The British printer, engraver, and satiric poet Thomas Hood (1799–1845) published "The Song of the Shirt" anonymously in the December 1843 issue of *Punch*, the poem having been inspired, he later said, by an incident which had drawn public attention to the appalling conditions faced by some workers in London. A woman with a starving infant at her breast "was charged at the Lambeth Police-court with pawning her master's goods, for which she had to give two pounds security. Her husband had died by an accident, and left her with two children to support, and she obtained by her needle for the maintenance of herself and family what her master called the good living of seven shillings a week." The words "Work,—work,—work" appear nine times in the poem's ten eight-line stanzas describing the misery and monotony of a factory seamstress's life, the eleventh and final stanza containing an additional (ninth) line to drive home the point of the woman's song: "Would that its tone could reach the Rich!"

5. Thoreau was at this time reading William Ward (1769–1823), *A View of the History, Literature, and Mythology of the Hindoos* (Seram-

pore, 1818), which contains the following sentence: "The fixing of the mind, so that it may not wander beyond the nose, nor descend inwardly beyond the level of the navel, is called *dharunu*, in which the yogee purifies his mind by benevolence . . . subdues all his members, and all the power of the elements over him."

6. Michael Flannery (1800–1900), called by a friend of Thoreau's "the industrious Irishman from Kerry," a county in southwest Ireland, had won the second premium of four dollars in the spading competition at the Middlesex Agricultural Fair in Concord, Massachusetts, on September 5, 1853. Incredibly, however, his employer, farmer Abiel H. Wheeler, received the prize money from the judges and kept it for himself, which infuriated Thoreau when he heard about it on October 12. Thoreau immediately wrote a subscription letter and carried it around to his neighbors asking them to contribute funds to make up the sum for Flannery, who had been saving money to bring his wife, Ann, and their two other children over from Ireland. (Flannery's eldest son accompanied his father to America.) Flannery shortly thereafter began working for dairy farmer Elijah Wood, who is the farmer Thoreau describes in this letter. In February 1854 Thoreau and Emerson loaned Flannery enough money to pay for his family's passage from Ireland. Flannery appears to have paid off the loan to Emerson, just five dollars, but Thoreau's sister Sophia found "a small note of hand" among Thoreau's papers after his death, which note she left with a friend of Thoreau's when she moved to Maine years later, telling the friend "to receive payment if [Flannery] was able to pay, but in any case to give him up the note," which the friend said he did.

7. Thoreau's common routine was to read and write in the mornings and evenings, and to walk into the woods and fields of Concord in the afternoons, although on occasion he instead surveyed in the afternoons. In Greek mythology, Zeus commanded Apollo, who had killed the Cyclopes, to serve as a herdsman to King Admetus.

8. This couplet is Thoreau's own.

9. The yew (*Taxus baccata, taxus* being Latin for "bow") was formerly much valued in archery for the making of long bows.

10. From December 19 to 21, 1853, Thoreau surveyed a small woodlot for James P. Brown, who was selling the property to William Wheeler.

11. Thoreau had read the three-volume *Life of Benjamin Robert Haydon, Historical Painter, from His Autobiography and Journals*, which had been edited and compiled by Tom Taylor and published in London earlier that year (1853).

12. I reprint from *Discoveries among the Ruins of Nineveh and Babylon; with Travels in Armenia, Kurdistan, and the Desert* (1853) by Sir Austen Henry Layard (1817–1894) the paragraph introducing the letter Thoreau speaks of and the entire letter itself, which appears at the very end of the volume, just before the "Appendix" (pp. 565–66):

In these pages I have occasionally indulged in reflections suggested by the scenes I have had to describe, and have ventured to point out the moral of the strange tale I have had to relate. I cannot better conclude than by showing the spirit in which Eastern philosophy and Mussulman resignation contemplate the evidences of ancient greatness and civilisation, suddenly rising up in the midst of modern ignorance and decay. A letter in my possession contained so true and characteristic a picture of the feelings that such an event excites in the mind of a good Mohammedan, that I here give a literal translation of its contents. It was written to a friend of mine by a Turkish Cadi, in reply to some inquiries as to the commerce, population, and remains of antiquity of an ancient city, in which dwelt the head of the law. These are its words:—

"My illustrious Friend, and Joy of my Liver!
"The thing you ask of me is both difficult and useless. Although I have passed all my days in this place, I have neither counted the houses nor have I inquired into the number of the inhabitants; and as to what one person loads on his mules and the other stows away in the bottom of his ship, that is no business of mine. But, above all, as to the previous

history of this city, God only knows the amount of dirt and confusion that the infidels may have eaten before the coming of the sword of Islam. It were unprofitable for us to inquire into it.

"Oh, my soul! oh, my lamb! seek not after the things which concern thee not. Thou camest unto us, and we welcomed thee: go in peace.

"Of a truth, thou hast spoken many words; and there is no harm done, for the speaker is one and the listener is another. After the fashion of thy people thou hast wandered from one place to another until thou art happy and content in none. We (praise be to God) were born here, and never desire to quit it. Is it possible then that the idea of a general intercourse between mankind should make any impression on our understandings? God forbid!

"Listen, oh my son! There is no wisdom equal unto the belief in God! He created the world, and shall we liken ourselves unto him in seeking to penetrate into the mysteries of his creation? Shall we say, behold this star spinneth round that star, and this other star with a tail goeth and cometh in so many years! Let it go! He from whose hand it came will guide and direct it.

"But thou wilt say unto me, Stand aside, oh man, for I am more learned than thou art, and have seen more things. If thou thinkest that thou art in this respect better than I am, thou art welcome. I praise God that I seek not that which I require not. Thou art learned in the things I care not for; and as for that which thou hast seen, I defile it. Will much knowledge create thee a double belly, or wilt thou seek Paradise with thine eyes?

"Oh, my friend! If thou wilt be happy, say, There is no God but God! Do no evil, and thus wilt thou fear neither man nor death; for surely thine hour will come!

"The meek in spirit (El Fakir),
"IMAUM ALI ZADÈ."

13. Part of the "go-ahead" lexicon of Thoreau's time. In the "Sunday" chapter of *A Week*, Thoreau quotes a peddler who once told him, " 'The way to trade . . . is to *put it right through*,' no matter what it is, anything that is agreed on."

14. Thoreau refers to the Brahmins mentioned in the first section of this letter and is thinking particularly of a quotation by Warren Hastings (1732–1818) that he read in the *Bhăgvat-Gēētā, or Dialogues of Krēēshnă and Ărjŏŏn* (London, 1785), translated by Charles Wilkins (1750–1836). Thoreau used the quotation in the "Monday" chapter of *A Week*, prefacing it with a brief remark. Both his remark and the quotation follow here:

Speaking of the spiritual discipline to which the Brahmans subjected themselves, and the wonderful power of abstraction to which they attained, instances of which had come under his notice, Hastings says:—

"To those who have never been accustomed to the separation of the mind from the notices of the senses, it may not be easy to conceive by what means such a power is to be attained; since even the most studious men of our hemisphere will find it difficult so to restrain their attention, but that it will wander to some object of present sense or recollection; and even the buzzing of a fly will sometimes have the power to disturb it. But if we are told that there have been men who were successively, for ages past, in the daily habit of abstracted contemplation, begun in the earliest period of youth, and continued in many to the maturity of age, each adding some portion of knowledge to the store accumulated by his predecessors; it is not assuming too much to conclude, that as the mind ever gathers strength, like the body, by exercise, so in such an exercise it may in each have acquired the faculty to which they aspired, and that their collective studies may have led them to the discovery of new tracks and combinations of sentiment, totally different from the doctrines with which the learned of other nations are acquainted; doctrines which, however speculative and subtle, still as they possess the advantage of being derived from a source so free from every adventitious mixture, may be equally founded in truth with the most simple of our own."

15. Peter of Amiens (ca. 1050–1115), also called Peter the Hermit (for instance, by Thoreau in his essay "Walking"), was a French monk who led the First Crusade to conquer the Holy Land.

16. This phrase—made popular by Davy Crockett (1786–1836),

whose personal motto was "Be sure you are right, and then go ahead"—was ubiquitous in antebellum America. Initially used to describe the upbeat optimism of the early Republic's inhabitants, during the 1850s the phrase increasingly took on a satiric cast, suggesting that Americans were chauvinistic and overly engrossed in commercial concerns. This shift is evident in "The Adventures of Gilbert Go-Ahead" by Samuel Griswold Goodrich (1793–1860; pen name: Peter Parley), a serial which ran in the popular children's monthly *Robert Merry's Museum* from January 1851 until it ended abruptly with the March 1856 publication of *The Voyages, Travels, and Adventures of Gilbert Go-Ahead in Foreign Parts*. Initially Gilbert Go-Ahead is a fairly attractive protagonist, but gradually he becomes more ominous, talking blithely about annexing other countries and becoming enmeshed in shady financial dealings.

Letter Fifteen

1. Alfred Guillaume Gabriel, Count d'Orsay (1801–1852), was a famous French dandy and wit, as well as being an accomplished painter and sculptor, although "wanting in the finish that can only be reached by persistent discipline." In 1827 he married Lady Harriet Gardiner, the daughter of his good friend Lord Blessington, and while the couple resided in London (1829–49) their residence was a resort of fashionable literary and artistic society. But they lived beyond their means, went bankrupt, and removed to Paris, where his wife soon died and he attempted to earn a living by painting portraits.

2. In classical mythology, Hercules and his wife Deianeira needed to cross a swollen river. Hercules swam across but left Deianeira to be ferried across by a centaur boatman, who attempted to rape her, whereupon Hercules shot the centaur with a poisoned arrow. The dying centaur exacted his revenge by offering Deianeira his blood, promising that it would act as a love ointment to keep her husband faithful to her. Suspecting one day that Hercules was interested in another woman, she gave him a shirt on which she

had spread some of the dying centaur's blood. The blood was poison, however, and began burning Hercules' flesh. Because he could not die, he built himself a funeral pyre, spread his cloak on the pyre, and lay down on it. The flames burned up the mortal part of him, while the immortal part ascended to Mount Olympus, where Zeus set him among the stars.

3. Thoreau had received a summons from the justice of the peace of Middlesex County, L. Marett, ordering him to appear before the justices of the Court of Common Pleas at Cambridge, the county seat, at 9 a.m. on January 20 in order to testify in the plea of tort between Leonard Spaulding Lots, plaintiff, and William C. Benjamin, the case relating to whether Benjamin exceeded his privilege in damming Concord River to a certain height, which resulted in flood-damaged crops upriver. Spaulding had filed the suit in February 1853, and Benjamin had hired Thoreau to check the height of the dam.

4. Shakespeare, *The Tempest* (1611), act 2, scene 2, line 42: "Misery acquaints a man with strange bedfellows."

5. James Riley (1777–1840), *An Authentic Narrative of the Loss of the American Brig Commerce, Wrecked on the Western Coast of Africa, in the Month of August, 1815, with an Account of the Sufferings of the Surviving Officers and Crew, Who Were Enslaved by the Wandering Arabs, on the African Desert, or Zahahrah; and Observations Historical, Geographical, &c. Made During the Travels of the Author, while a Slave to the Arabs, and in the Empire of Morocco . . . Illustrated and Embellished with Ten Copperplate Engravings; Revised, and His Life Continued, by the Author, in January,* 1828 (Hartford, Conn.: Judd, Loomis, 1836).

6. Pigeon hawk (*Falco columbarius*), which Thoreau contrasts to the "squab," or fledgling pigeon, later in the sentence.

7. A pun, of course, on the Middlesex County Court of Common Pleas.

Letter Sixteen

1. An allusion to the poem of 1807 by English poet William Wordsworth (1770–1850) "The World Is Too Much with Us,"

which begins, "The world is too much with us; late and soon, / Getting and spending, we lay waste our powers; / Little we see in Nature that is ours; / We have given our hearts away, a sordid boon!"

2. Hosea 8:7, "For they have sown the wind, and they shall reap the whirlwind. . . ."

3. Effervescing salts (so called from the resemblance to the natural water of Seidlitz, Bohemia) consisting of two separate powders, one of which contained sodium bicarbonate, tartrate of potassium, and sodium, and the other tartaric acid. The powders are mixed in water, and drunk while effervescing as a mild cathartic.

4. Although this has all the earmarks of a colloquial expression, I have been unable to find a record of such an expression.

5. In part I, stage 7, of Bunyan's *The Pilgrim's Progress,* the pilgrims Christian and Hopeful trespass on the grounds of Giant Despair, who lives in Doubting Castle and is married to Diffidence. The two pilgrims are imprisoned in the dungeon, where Giant Despair soundly thrashes them, encourages them to commit suicide, and repeatedly threatens them with death by dismemberment—all largely at the behest of Diffidence. Finally Christian realizes that he has a key in his bosom called Promise, which he uses to effect his and Hopeful's escape from the domain of Giant Despair.

6. Doubtless Ralph Waldo Emerson is referred to here.

7. In August 1855 the firm Clarke & White of Saratoga Springs, New York, which owned Congress Spring and sold Congress Water from that spring, launched an enormous advertising campaign in an attempt to regain losses it had suffered to competitors in the highly lucrative mineral-water market. The firm sent hundreds of thousands of flyers and broadsides all over the United States and Canada, in both English and (for Quebec) French, the materials attesting to the product being "peculiarly beneficial as a general preservative of the tone of the stomach, and of the purity of the blood, removing by its aperient and alterative effects all predisposition to *fevers, bilious* or *liver* complaints." To support these claims, the materials also provided analyses of

Congress Water by the American chemist Dr. John H. Steele and British chemists Sir Humphry Davy and Dr. Michael Faraday. That month the firm also filed suit in the Southern New York District Court against several of its competitors, submitting sets of the flyers and broadsides to support its case.

8. Inactivity, indolence.

9. Possibly an allusion to John Milton (1608–1674), "L'Allegro," line 80: "The cynosure of neighbouring eyes."

10. During his Egyptian campaign of 1798–99, General Napoleon Bonaparte had crossed the Red Sea dry-shod at low tide on the morning of December 28, 1798, in order to visit the Wells of Moses. When he returned that evening, his party attempted a crossing at a lower part of the sea, but the tide was coming in, which threw them into disorder, at which point Napoleon ordered his horsemen to find shallower water so that they could complete the crossing.

11. This is actually a widening of the Sudbury River two miles south of Concord, Massachusetts, and half a mile southwest of Walden Pond.

12. 1 Timothy 6:12, "Fight the good fight of faith, lay hold on eternal life, whereunto thou art also called, and hast professed a good profession before many witnesses."

13. This may be a turn on "Giant Despair" from Bunyan's *The Pilgrim's Progress*, but I can shed no further light on Thoreau's intention.

14. Thoreau mentions this fact in Letter 10 as well. I have not been able to locate his source.

15. In his journal entry of June 13, 1854, Thoreau mentions seeing a group of "farmers in small parties, busily hoeing corn and potatoes. . . . They have a jug of sweetened water in the grass at the end of the row."

Letter Seventeen

1. As the next letter indicates, Blake spoke of an excursion to Mount Wachusett, twenty-six miles west of Concord and sixteen miles north of downtown Worcester.

2. Thoreau's former Harvard schoolmate Benjamin Marston Watson (1820–1896) had written on September 17 that he and a few of Thoreau's other friends in Plymouth "have clubbed together and raised a small sum in hope of persuading you to come down and read them a paper or two some Sunday. They can offer you $10 at least." Thoreau wrote back on September 19 and proposed Sunday, October 1.
3. Thoreau had agreed to deliver his lecture "The Wild" on November 21 at Philadelphia's Spring Garden Institute, which was founded in 1850 to give technical training to young men.

Letter Twenty

1. During the preceding twenty-six months Thoreau had read ten of the Harvard College Library's thirty-five volumes of the *Jesuit Relations*—annual accounts written by Jesuit missionaries in Canada to their superiors in France between 1633 and 1672. These volumes contain harrowing accounts of several Indians and a few of the missionaries being burned at the stake.
2. A frequent admonition in the Old Testament. See, for instance, Deuteronomy 31:6, "Be strong and of a good courage, fear not, nor be afraid of them: for the Lord thy God, he it is that doth go with thee; he will not fail thee, nor forsake thee."
3. In classical mythology, Atlas was a Titan and an ally of Kronos in the war against Zeus, who punished him for his rebellion by condemning him to bear the heavens upon his shoulders.
4. Latin and Greek, the sense of which is "a subtraction, not an addition, and therefore not a burden."
5. Probably Thoreau had in mind here such "disciplines" as he saw performed in the Cathedral of Notre Dame in Montreal, where "a troop of Canadians" entered "and one and all kneeled down in the aisle before the high altar to their devotions, somewhat awkwardly, as cattle prepare to lie down. . . ."
6. To get a sense of who this neighbor might be, it may be useful to consult the "Solitude" chapter of *Walden*: "For the most part

we allow only outlying and transient circumstances to make our occasions. They are, in fact, the cause of our distraction. Nearest to all things is that power which fashions their being. *Next* to us the grandest laws are continually being executed. *Next* to us is not the workman whom we have hired, with whom we love so well to talk, but the workman whose work we are."

7. The 1850 U.S. Census forms had a column for "deaf and dumb, blind, insane, idiotic, pauper or convict"; the census taker in Concord listed two deaf and dumb, one blind, five insane, one idiotic, eight paupers, and five convicts among the 2,249 residents.

8. In 1849 French army captain Claude Étienne Minié (1814–1879) invented the rifle that was named after him. Weighing almost eleven pounds, it had a percussion lock and fired a 500-grain conical .702 caliber bullet with a cavity in its base plugged with a piece of iron. By the explosion of the charge, the iron plug was driven further in, expanding the sides to fit closely the grooves of the barrel. The rifle was reasonably accurate at up to six hundred yards and could penetrate four inches of soft pine at one thousand yards. The Minié rifle saw its first widescale use during the Crimean War, the *"Eastern War"* Thoreau mentions, which began in October 1853, when Turkey declared war on Russia. Great Britian and France joined the war against Russia in March 1854, in large part in response to the destruction of the Turkish fleet at Sinope in November 1853. Allied troops commanded by Britain's Lord Raglan and France's Marshal Saint-Arnaud invaded Crimea in September 1854 near the port of Sevastopol, the home of Russia's Black Sea fleet. On September 20 Prince Menchikoff, the Russian commander and son of Emperor Nicholas I, tried to hold the Sevastopol road on the heights of the river Alma but was forced to retreat; and five days later the allies held the harbors of Kamiesh and Balaklava, from which they laid siege to Sevastopol. On October 25 Lord Cardigan led the famous charge of the Light Brigade at Balaklava, and the Battle of Inkermann took place on November 5, the allies losing 3,300 men and the Rus-

sians losing 12,000. The Crimean War, which cost the allies 252,600 mean and the Russians 256,000 men, continued until March 1856 with the signing of the Treaty of Paris.

9. Daniel Tarbell (1801–1883), the deacon in the Second Congregational Church of Concord and a farmer, lived on the Old Marlboro Road in Concord, Massachusetts.

10. 2 Corinthians 5:10, "For we must all appear before the judgment seat of Christ; that every one may receive the things done in his body, according to that he hath done, whether it be good or bad."

Letter Twenty-two

1. An echo of Exodus 20:7, "Thou shalt not take the name of the Lord thy God in vain; for the Lord will not hold him guiltless that taketh his name in vain."

2. A medicinal concoction of bitter herbs, roots, and (often) alcohol.

3. A passenger boat carrying mail and cargo on a regular schedule.

4. William Lloyd Garrison (1805–1879) and Wendell Phillips (1811–1884) were the two best-known abolitionists in antebellum America. Garrison founded and edited *The Liberator*, a daily newspaper that was the principal organ of the American Anti-Slavery Society; Phillips, Garrison's close friend and colleague, achieved great fame as a rousing orator. Both men spoke at the annual meeting of the Middlesex County Anti-Slavery Society in the Concord Town Hall on Friday, June 29.

5. The letter Thoreau refers to and quotes from is dated only "Tuesday 1855," but since Thoreau responded to it on February 7, Cholmondeley probably wrote it on a Tuesday in late January. One portion of the letter that Thoreau may have been eager for Blake to read is Cholmondeley's remark, "Turn it how you will, our English nation *no longer stands upon the Living Laws of the Eternal God*—we have turned ourselves to an empire & cotton bags & the leprosy of prodigious manufacture. Let that all go & let us grow

great men again instead of dressing up dolls for the market. I feel we are strong enough to live a better life than this one which now festers in all our joints." Cholmondeley's book was *Ultima Thule; or, Thoughts Suggested by a Residence in New Zealand* (London, 1854).

Letter Twenty-five

1. The Indian name of the Concord River was Musketaquid, which means "grass-ground." Thoreau wrote in his first book, *A Week on the Concord and Merrimack Rivers*, that the Musketaquid "will be Grass-ground River as long as grass grows and water runs here; it will be Concord River only while men lead peaceable lives on its banks."

2. *The Task* (1784) by the English poet William Cowper (1731–1800) contains six books and almost five thousand lines. Ricketson told Thoreau in his letter of August 12, 1854, that *The Task* was his "greatest favorite" work of the English poets, asserted that "Cowper was a true lover of the country," and quoted three lines from the poem. The others mentioned are the Scottish poet James Thomson (1700–1748), best known for his four-part poem, *The Seasons* (London, 1730); English poet Thomas Gray (1716–1771), best known for his "Elegy Written in a Country Churchyard" (1751); and probably the Quaker author and poet William Howitt (1792–1879), best known as the author of *The Book of the Seasons* (London, 1831), but possibly his wife Mary Howitt (1799–1888), also a Quaker and perhaps best known for her poem "The Spider and the Fly" (ca. 1847).

3. John 6:35, "And Jesus said unto them, I am the bread of life: he that cometh to me shall never hunger; and he that believeth on me shall never thirst." See Letter 3 for an earlier treatment of this idea; for an extended treatment, see the "Economy" chapter of *Walden*.

4. This fit end to an incredible sentence may possibly be an allusion to Homer, the *Iliad*, book 12, line 243: "The single best augury is to fight for one's country."

5. Now more popularly called the three Rs: reading, writing, and 'rithmetic.

6. Minister, reformer, lecturer, and author Thomas Wentworth Higginson (1823–1911) and Theo Brown were accompanied on their trip to Mount Katahdin in central Maine by three other men and five women, the latter of whom wore bloomers, a novelty at that time. Higginson also insisted that the women wear boots on the trip. As he mentions in his 1898 autobiography, *Cheerful Yesterdays,* he wrote this journey up, adopting the persona of a woman and indeed making the entire party consist of ten women. The narrative appeared anonymously in the September 1856 *Putnam's Magazine* under the title "Going to Mount Katahdin." "Theo" is mentioned once in the story, however, and in the narrative Higginson quotes from Thoreau's "Ktaadn and the Maine Woods," which had been serialized (in five installments) in *Sartain's Union Magazine* during 1848.

7. See note 17 on "Delectable *Mts.*" in Letter 12.

8. A reference to the English poet Percy Bysshe Shelley's poem "Ozymandias," which relates a traveler's story of finding in the desert the ruins of a colossal statue with these words on the pedestal: "My name is Ozymandias, king of kings: / Look on my works, ye mighty, and despair!"

9. An allusion to English poet John Milton's "Epitaph on Shakespeare," the first four lines of which read: "What needs my Shakespeare for his honour'd bones,— / The labour of an age in piled stones? / Or that his hallow'd relics should be hid / Under a star-y-pointing pyramid?"

Letter Twenty-six

1. The following sentence from the "Reading" chapter of *Walden* gives a sense of Thoreau's intention: "The oldest Egyptian or Hindoo philosopher raised a corner of the veil from the statue of the divinity; and still the trembling robe remains raised, and I

gaze upon as fresh a glory as he did, since it was I in him that was then so bold, and it is he in me that now reviews the vision."

2. Revelation 22:17, "And the Spirit and the bride say, Come. And let him that is athirst come. And whosoever will, let him take the water of life freely." The Ganges or Ganga River figures so prominently in Indian myth, religion, and history that Prime Minister Jawaharlal Nehru (1889–1964) called it the "symbol of India's age-long culture and civilization."

3. In Greek mythology, the place where virtuous people went after death.

4. Philippians 4:7, "And the peace of God, which passeth all understanding, shall keep your hearts and minds through Jesus Christ."

5. Possibly another allusion (see note 8 to Letter 8, "Pierian spring") to Alexander Pope's "Essay on Criticism": "A little learning is a dangerous thing; / Drink deep, or taste not the Pierian spring. . . ."

6. The downtown shopping area along Main Street in Concord, Massachusetts, named for the dam (of a mill) that once backed up a stream running under the area.

7. A Thracian poet who could move even inanimate things by his music. When his wife Eurydice died, he went into the infernal regions and so charmed King Pluto that Eurydice was released from death on the condition that Orpheus would not look back until he reached the earth. He was just about to place his foot on the earth when he turned around, and Eurydice vanished from him in an instant.

8. In his journal entry for November 9, the day he went wooding with Blake on the Assabet River, he wrote, "Found a good stone jug, small size, floating stopple up. I drew the stopple and smelled, as I expected, molasses and water, or something stronger (black-strap?), which it had contained. Probably some meadow haymakers' jug left in the grass, which the recent rise of the river has floated off. It will do to put with the white pitcher I found and keep flowers in. Thus I get my furniture."

9. Thoreau had something of a reputation for nighttime excursions

on the river, during which he would build a fire on a grate mounted to the front of his boat, the fire illuminating the bottom of the river.

10. Although this has all the earmarks of a proverbial expression, I was unable to locate a record of such an expression in any of several dictionaries of proverbs.

11. Mary Moody Emerson (1774–1863) was Ralph Waldo Emerson's deeply religious paternal aunt.

12. Thoreau biographer Walter Harding tells the story well: "In the autumn of 1855 Cholmondeley gathered up a collection of forty-four Oriental books, including translations of the *Rig Veda Sanhita,* the *Mandukya Upanishads,* the *Nala* and *Damyanta,* the *Vishnu Purana,* the *Institutes of Menu,* the *Sankhya Karika,* the *Aphorisms of the Mimasma* and *Nayaya,* the *Bhagavat Gheeta, Sakoontala,* and the *Bhagavita Purana* as well as a number of volumes of history and criticism of Indian literature, and shipped them to Thoreau as a token of friendship. When Thoreau learned of their imminent arrival, he gathered up appropriate pieces of driftwood along the Concord rivers to make a special bookcase. When they arrived in Concord on November 30, he made haste to write Cholmondeley:

> After overhauling my treasures on the carpet, wading knee deep in Indian philosophy and poetry—with eager eyes around ready to admire the splendid binding and illumination at least, drawing them forth necessarily from amidst a heap of papers . . . I placed them in the case which I had prepared, and went late to bed dreaming of what had happened. Indeed it was exactly like the realization of some dreams which I have had; but when I woke in the morning I was not convinced that it was reality until I peeped out and saw their bright backs.

"Thoreau sent Cholmondeley a copy of Emerson's *Poems, Walden,* a book by F[rederick] L[aw] Olmsted [1822–1903] on the South, and a first edition of Whitman's *Leaves of Grass* in return and wrote boastfully to Ricketson of Cholmondeley's 'royal gift': 'I send you information of this as I might the birth of a child.'"

Letter Twenty-seven

1. On October 25, 1855, Thoreau responded to a letter from the
   Reverend James Colder (1826–1893; also spelled "Calder") by
   offering to lecture in Harrisburg, Pennsylvania, on either January
   9 or 16, 1856. Colder had been a Methodist Episcopal mis-
   sionary in China from July 1851 to April 1854, but in April
   1855 he had become pastor of the Fourth Street Bethel (Church
   of God) in Harrisburg, which did not formally open its doors
   until construction was completed on November 4, 1855, just
   ten days after Thoreau's letter to Colder. No letters from Colder
   to Thoreau survive.

2. Blake had apparently suggested a walk to Mount Asnebumskit,
   six miles over crusted snow each way from Blake's house. Later
   in this letter Thoreau says such a walk was "tempting to think
   of. . . . But—but—"

3. From "Chapter XII: The Walk to Dummer," in *Roughing It in the
   Bush* (London, 1852) by Susanna Strickland Moodie
   (1803–1884): "Old Jenny and I were left alone with the little
   children, in the depths of the dark forest, to help ourselves in the
   best way we could. Men could not be procured in that thinly-
   settled spot for love nor money, and I now fully realised the
   extent of Jenny's usefulness. Daily she yoked the oxen, and
   brought down from the bush fuel to maintain our fires, which
   she felled and chopped up with her own hands. She fed the cattle, and kept all things snug about the doors. . . ."

4. Two hints for interpreting this symbol: Letter 12, where
   Thoreau writes, "[I]f you will look at another star I will try to
   supply my side of the triangle"; and Letter 25, where he writes,
   "We will stand on solid foundations to one another,—a column
   planted on this shore, you on that. We meet the same sun in his
   rising. We were built slowly, and have come to our bearing. We
   will not mutually fall over that we may meet, but will grandly and
   eternally guard the straits."

5. In 1832 the Boston publisher C. Gaylord issued *The Letter Writer:*

Containing a Great Variety of Letters on the Following Subjects: Relationship, Business, Love, Courtship, and Marriage, Friendship, and Miscellaneous Letters, Law Forms, &c., &c. Selected from Judicious and Eminent Writers. The following year the G. and C. Merriam Company of Springfield, Massachusetts, published the first book in its popular "Letter Writer" series, *The Fashionable American Letter Writer; or, The Art of Polite Correspondence.* . . .

6. Dissipation was thought to give everything a blue tinge, so "blue" means tipsy. A couplet published in *Fraser's Magazine* (London) in 1838 expresses the idea nicely: "Drink till all is blue. / Cracking bottles till all is blue."

7. Each March and April most newspapers in and around New England ran articles about the maple sugar season. Thoreau quoted one such article in the *New-York Weekly Tribune* of April 24, 1857, for instance, in his journal entry of the following day.

8. In 1846 Tom Smith, a London confectioner, first began selling candies wrapped in "mottoes," or love notes, around each of which was a twist of bright-colored paper. Confectioners in the United States soon began manufacturing their own versions of these popular candies. In 1866 Daniel Chase, brother of Oliver Chase, who had founded the Boston-based New England Confectionery Company (NECCO) in 1847, invented a process for printing these "mottoes" directly onto candy wafers.

9. Alternate spelling for "Asnebumskit," the hill in Paxton, Massachusetts, mentioned in Letter 10.

10. Diamonds, before the discovery of the American and African mines, were found only in certain districts of central India. The world's most famous and infamous diamonds, such as the Koh-i-Noor, the Hope, and the Regent, were mined in the kingdom of Golconda.

11. The British librarian and poet Coventry Kersey Dighton Patmore (1823–1896) married Emily Augusta Andrews (1824–1862) in 1847 and, believing her to be the perfect Victorian wife, wrote the four-book epic poem *The Angel in the House*

to celebrate her virtues in particular (in the guise of a character named Honoria) and married love in general. The first book, *The Betrothal*, was published anonymously in London in 1854. Concurrent with the 1856 London publication of the second book, *The Espousals*, the Boston firm of Ticknor and Fields published the first two books in separate volumes, which became extraordinarily popular in the United States and which in turn spurred Patmore's fame in England, even winning him the praise of such eminent poets and writers as Alfred, Lord Tennyson (1809–1892), Robert Browning (1812–1889), and Thomas Carlyle (1795–1881). The final two books of the epic were published in 1860 (*Faithful for Ever*) and 1863 (*Victories of Love*).

Letter Twenty-eight

1. Blake had probably suggested an excursion to the town of Harvard, Massachusetts, which is twelve miles west of Concord and nineteen miles northeast of Worcester, although he may have suggested an excursion to Harvard College in Cambridge.

2. Although Thoreau may refer here to a remark in Blake's letter, the basis for the dispute may have been the "Solitude" chapter of *Walden*, where Thoreau assesses both solitude and society—and displays a clear bias for the former.

3. The refrain from the hymn "Don't You See My Jesus Coming?" by Isaac Watts (1674–1748), published in *Hymns and Spiritual Songs* (Geneva, N.Y., 1812), is "I am bound for the kingdom, / Will you go to glory with me? / Hallelujah! O praise ye the Lord."

4. The *New-York Tribune*, published by Horace Greeley, was the most popular newspaper in the United States during the 1850s. The Sermon on the Mount, related in Matthew 5–7, was the major event in Jesus's ministry and contains what may be called a précis of Christianity's moral imperatives.

Letter Thirty

1. Napoleon Bonaparte said at the end of December 1815, while dictating his memoirs, published in the 1823 edition of *Mémorial de Ste-Hélène*, "As to moral courage, I have rarely met with two o'clock in the morning courage; I mean instantaneous courage." Thoreau also used his "3 o'clock" version of Bonaparte's quotation in the "Sounds" chapter of his book *Walden* and in his famous essay "Walking."

2. While visiting Brown on October 24, Thoreau had borrowed from him a copy of the September 1856 *Putnam's Magazine,* which featured Thomas Wentworth Higginson's article "Going to Mount Katahdin" (see note 6 to Letter 25).

3. The *Worcester Daily Transcript*, one of the city's two daily newspapers, was edited at this time by Zebina K. Pangborn (b. 1829).

4. A horse with a racking gait, which is to say a fast four-beat gait in which each hoof touches the ground separately and at equal intervals.

5. Whitman had self-published the first edition of *Leaves of Grass* in July 1855. That edition contained twelve untitled poems and a frontispiece portrait of the poet. The second edition of *Leaves of Grass* was self-published in 1856 and contained, in addition to thirty-two poems, now with titles, a forty-two-page appendix of reviews of the first edition titled "Leaves-Droppings," which included a laudatory letter from Ralph Waldo Emerson in response to receiving a complimentary copy of the first edition. Whitman had not secured Emerson's permission to publish the letter and, incredibly, even printed a quote from the letter ("I Greet You at the Beginning of A Great Career R W Emerson") on the spine of the book.

6. "Poem of Walt Whitman, an American" (later retitled "Song of Myself") and "Sun-Down Poem" (later retitled "Crossing Brooklyn Ferry") appeared in the second edition.

7. Near the end of his essay "Succession of Forest Trees," Thoreau wrote, "Though I do not believe that a plant will spring up where

no seed has been, I have great faith in a seed—a, to me, equally mysterious origin for it. Convince me that you have a seed there, and I am prepared to expect wonders."

Letter Thirty-one

1. David Atwood Wasson (1823–1887) was a prominent minister, essayist, and poet. He was at this time minister of the South Congregational (Unitarian) Church in Boston, but in the spring of 1857 he visited Worcester for an extended period, later taking up full-time residence in the city.
2. Possibly an echo of Mark 8:36–37, "For what shall it profit a man, if he gain the whole world, and lose his own soul? Or what shall a man give in exchange for his soul?"
3. Thoreau did in fact write such a lecture, "Autumnal Tints," which he first delivered in Worcester on February 22, 1859. In the spring of 1862, just before his death, Thoreau culled an essay from the much larger manuscript he called *The Fall of the Leaf* and submitted that essay to his publisher with the title "Autumnal Tints." The essay appeared in the October 1862 *Atlantic Monthly*, five months after Thoreau's death.
4. From Ellery Channing's poem "Baker Farm," which first appeared in Channing's collection *The Woodman, and Other Poems* (Boston, 1849): "Pan of unwrinkled cream, / May some poet dash thee in his churn!"

Letter Thirty-three

1. The fruit of the celtis or hackberry (*Celtis occidentalis*), which encloses a pit (seed) usually less than a quarter of an inch in diameter, matures in September and October.
2. Edward Everett Hale (1822–1909) was a teacher, author, editor, and minister as well as an amateur naturalist. He is now best

known for his short story "The Man without a Country," published in the *Atlantic Monthly* of December 1863.

3. Seth Rogers (1823–1893) was a physician from Vermont who moved to Worcester in 1850, established a general practice, and shortly afterward founded the Worcester Water Cure. For David A. Wasson, see note 1 to Letter 31.

4. Thoreau had received a letter from Cholmondeley dated February 22, 1857, but because this letter is not especially long and mentions nothing about sending more books, Thoreau must refer to a later one that has not survived.

5. Letter 41 indicates that Blake and Ricketson did not meet until late in 1858.

6. At this time Channing was employed as a journalist in New Bedford.

Letter Thirty-six

1. Probably "XVth ly" is simply an expression Thoreau uses for picking up the thread from the last letter. In the "Sunday" chapter of *A Week*, he quotes several passages of scripture from the New Testament and then writes, "Think of repeating these things to a New England audience! thirdly, fourthly, fifteenthly, till there are three barrels of sermons! Who, without cant, can read them aloud?"

2. Sufficient forward speed to enable a vessel to be steered with a rudder.

3. A drag sail is rigged to a stout frame and dragged by a vessel through the water in order to prevent drifting, but Thoreau here probably refers to the setting of stay sails fore and aft, which have the combined effect of keeping a vessel more or less stationary.

4. Joseph Polis (sometimes "Porus") was an accomplished Penobscot Indian chief who had represented his tribe in political and religious matters as early as 1842. The editor of the *Boston Recorder* was so impressed with Polis that he published an article titled "Progress of Civilization" about him, highlighting Polis's determination to

educate himself, on January 11, 1844. Thoreau's own account of Polis in *The Maine Woods* is highly laudatory, in part because Thoreau saw Polis as a man who succeeded in retaining his Indian ways while accommodating himself to the larger culture.

5. As Joseph J. Moldenhauer has written, Thoreau and Hoar "walked 'five miles through a swamp' on the Mud Pond Carry, on July 27. Portaging from Umbazookskus Lake (in the Penobscot drainage) to Mud Pond (a source of the Allegash), Thoreau and Hoar lost their way. They struggled through swamps to Chamberlain Lake, below Mud Pond, where they rejoined Polis and their canoe. . . . 'We had expected to ascend [Mount Katahdin] from this point, but my companion was obliged to give up this on account of sore feet.' Though Hoar could have waited for them at Hunt's Farm, Thoreau and Polis did not undertake an ascent of the mountain. After the rigors of the preceding week Thoreau was doubtless weary; and Polis fell ill that evening with severe 'colic.' Thoreau had climbed Katahdin via the southern approach on his first Maine excursion eleven years before."

6. In the first chapter of *The Maine Woods*, Thoreau thus extolled the virtues of a locally brewed beer he was given while deep in the woods: "It was as if we sucked at the very teats of Nature's pine-clad bosom in these parts,—the sap of all Millinocket botany commingled,—the topmost, most fantastic, and spiciest sprays of the primitive wood, and whatever invigorating and stringent gum or essence it afforded steeped and dissolved in it,—a lumberer's drink, which would acclimate and naturalize a man at once,—which would make him see green, and, if he slept, dream that he heard the wind sough among the pines."

Letter Thirty-seven

1. Thoreau's source for this statistic has not been located. In the "Economy" chapter of *Walden* he writes, "What has been said of the merchants, that a very large majority, even ninety-seven in a hundred, are sure to fail, is equally true of the farmers." In his

essay "Life without Principle" he also uses the latter figure: "You must get your living by loving. But as it is said of the merchants that ninety-seven in a hundred fail, so the life of men generally, tried by this standard, is a failure, and bankruptcy may be surely prophesied."

2. Psalm 97:1, "The Lord reigneth; let the earth rejoice; let the multitude of isles be glad thereof."

3. Transcendentalism, or "the Newness," as it developed in the 1830s and continued till the Civil War was regarded by many in the United States as "moonshine"—foolishness of thought, nonsense.

4. Matthew 11:7, "And as they departed, Jesus began to say unto the multitudes concerning John, What went ye out into the wilderness to see? A reed shaken by the wind?"

5. Kansas became a territory of the United States in 1854, but the populace was deeply divided on the issue of slavery. A proslavery legislature expelled antislavery members on July 2, 1855, so the antislavery faction met the following month and quickly hammered out the Topeka Constitution, which was adopted on November 2, 1855. President Pierce rejected that constitution, however, stating that the framers did not constitute a body politic. The proslavery Lecompton Constitution was adopted on November 7, 1857, resulting in a political stalemate because by this time the antislavery faction controlled the territorial legislature.

6. The French socialist reformer François Marie Charles Fourier (1772–1837) proposed to improve the human condition by reorganizing society into communities. Most of the experimental utopian communities set up in the United States during the antebellum period operated under Fourierite principles. One such community was Brook Farm (1841–47), organized by George Ripley (1802–1880) on a 178-acre farm in West Roxbury, Massachusetts, six miles southwest of Boston. This and all the other utopian communities of the time failed, as Thoreau mentions.

7. To "go to board" means either to take regular meals at or to lodge and take regular meals at an establishment such as a boardinghouse.

8. One "keeps house" by providing for one's own lodging and dining.

9. On September 12, 1857, the side-wheel steamer SS *Central America* sank off the North Carolina coast in a hurricane. Of the 578 passengers and crew who had embarked from Havana four days before, only 153 survived, making this the worst peacetime disaster at sea in American history. Most of the passengers were returning via the Isthmus of Panama from the gold fields of California, many of them loaded with gold-filled money belts. Also on board were twenty-one tons of California gold valued at $1.6 million and bound for the U.S. Treasury Department's assay office in New York City. The location of the ship was discovered at a depth of 8,500 feet in 1987, and in September 1989 a salvage operation led by Tommy Thompson recovered the gold using remote-controlled robots. *Life* magazine called it "the greatest treasure ever found."

10. John Ruskin (1819–1900) was an artist, scientist, poet, environmentalist, philosopher, and the preeminent art critic of his time. Throughout October and November 1857 Thoreau was reading the first four volumes of Ruskin's *Modern Painters* (1843–56), *Seven Lamps of Architecture* (1848), and *The Elements of Drawing* (1857). The "themes" Thoreau refers to are dealt with most directly in the second volume of *Modern Painters* (1846), where Ruskin presents, as George P. Landow writes, his "theories of imagination and his theocentric system of aesthetics by which he explains the nature of beauty and demonstrates its importance in human life. He combines a Coleridgean theory of imagination . . . with evangelical conceptions of biblical prophecy and divine inspiration. . . . All beauty, if properly regarded, is theophany, the revelation of God. Contemplating beauty, like contemplating the Bible, God's other revelation, is a moral and religious act." In his journal entry for October 29, Thoreau summarized what he

found uncongenial in Ruskin: "The love of Nature and fullest perception of the revelation which she is to man is not compatible with the belief in the peculiar revelation of the Bible which Ruskin entertains."

11. One of three tribes of South Africa, the Bushman and Bantu being the other two. Thoreau read about the Hottentots in Roualeyn Gordon-Cumming (1820–1866), *Five Years of a Hunter's Life in the Far Interior of Southern Africa* (1850), from which he picked up an anecdote that he uses in his essay "Walking." Thoreau clearly regarded the Hottentots as exemplars of wildness in human beings: "The Hottentots eagerly devour the marrow of the koodoo and other antelopes raw, as a matter of course. . . . Give me a Wildness whose glance no civilization can endure,—as if we lived on the marrow of koodoos devoured raw."

12. Blake had obviously purchased a map of the White Mountains and made an excursion there alone, probably walking the most popular route of the time, the Crawford Trail from the Crawford House at Crawford Notch to the summit (an eight-mile hike with an elevation gain of almost 4,400 feet) and then down to the Glen House below Pinkham Notch (eight miles if he followed the Glen Bridal Trail, with a descent of about 4,400 feet).

13. The first of the critical two questions Thoreau uses at the end of his famous "Contact" passage in the "Ktaadn" chapter of *The Maine Woods:* "I stand in awe of my body, this matter to which I am bound has become so strange to me. I fear not spirits, ghosts, of which I am one,—*that* my body might,—but I fear bodies, I tremble to meet them. What is this Titan that has possession of me? Talk of mysteries!—Think of our life in nature,—daily to be shown matter, to come in contact with it,—rocks, trees, wind on our cheeks! the *solid* earth! the *actual* world! the *common sense!* *Contact! Contact! Who* are we? *where* are we?" Contact with unmediated matter, "the *actual* world" (as here, atop a mountain), prompts in Thoreau the recognition that *who we are* is "spirits, ghosts" within bodies which enable us to have these fundamentally mysterious experiences of coming "in contact with" the

world of Nature. The body, then, for Thoreau, is a conduit between spirit and matter.

14. Mount Washington (elevation 6,288 feet) is the highest peak of the Presidential Range in the White Mountains. Mount Jefferson (5,715 feet), almost two and a half miles north of Mount Washington, is third highest. Mount Madison is seventh highest (5,363 feet) and is four and a third miles north of Mount Washington. Mount Lafayette (5,260 feet) rises above Franconia Notch, New Hampshire, eighteen miles southwest of Mount Washington.

15. Umbagog Lake straddles the border between New Hampshire and Maine 32 miles north-northeast of the summit of Mount Washington, whereas Moosehead Lake is fully 115 miles northeast of the summit. The Atlantic coast is about 65 miles southeast of the summit. Likely, then, Thoreau is correct in suggesting Blake saw Umbagog Lake from the summit.

16. Reinhold Solger (1817–1866) was a Prussian academic who had fled to Switzerland in 1848 after participating in the failed Rebellion of Baden in 1848. After immigrating to the United States in 1853, Solger made his living primarily by lecturing and reporting on international affairs for Boston newspapers. Franklin Benjamin Sanborn (1831–1917) had graduated from Harvard College in 1855 and for seven years operated a private preparatory school in Concord attended by the children of Emerson, Hawthorne, and other prominent families.

17. A Thoreauvian alteration of John 9:4, "I must work the works of him that sent me, while it is day: the night cometh, when no man can work."

18. Thoreau had attended an opera while visiting New York City in November 1854 but seems not to have been terribly impressed. In his journal entry of October 29, 1858, just two weeks before writing this letter, he wrote, "Who is the most profitable companion? He who has been picking cranberries and chopping wood, or he who has been attending the opera all his days? I find when I have been building a fence or surveying a farm, or even

collecting simples [medicinal herbs], that these were the true paths to perception and enjoyment. My being seems to have put forth new roots and to be more strongly planted. This is the true way to crack the nut of happiness."

19. Thoreau refers here to a printer's devil, usually the youngest apprentice in a printing office, who performs menial tasks such as washing ink rollers, sweeping, and—as in this instance—running errands.

Letter Forty-one

1. An allusion to *Sartor Resartus: The Life and Opinions of Herr Teufelsdröckh* (1831) by the Scottish historian, critic, and writer Thomas Carlyle (1795–1881). The book's protagonist, Diogenes Teufelsdröckh, lived at the fictional Weissnichtwo, German for "know-not-where."

2. Founded by Harvey D. Parker (d. 1884) in 1855, the Parker House was Boston's premier restaurant and hotel during Thoreau's time. Almost immediately after the establishment opened, a select group of Boston-area writers and intellectuals began meeting at the restaurant on the last Saturday afternoon of each month for readings, intellectual discussions, and fine food and drink. The group dubbed itself the Saturday Club, and was by far the longest lived and most famous of the many intellectually oriented social clubs that formed in the Boston area during the nineteenth century. The idea that resulted in the *Atlantic Monthly* magazine grew out of this club. Its members included such luminaries as Ralph Waldo Emerson, editor and poet James Russell Lowell (1819–1891), novelist Nathaniel Hawthorne (1804–1864), writer and physician Oliver Wendell Holmes (1809–1894), Harvard professor and scientist Louis Agassiz (1807–1873), and poets John Greenleaf Whittier (1807–1892) and Henry Wadsworth Longfellow (1807–1882). Thoreau refused to have anything whatever to do with this club.

3. A variant of the first few lines of "The Dragon of Wantley" (that is, Warncliff, in Yorkshire, England), a ballad describing a local hero (More) who had a suit of spiked armor made so that a dragon attacking him would be so harmed by the spikes that it would die—a scheme that worked. Thoreau likely was recalling the lines from memory, having read them thirteen years earlier (in 1846, while at Walden Pond) in Bishop Thomas Percy (1729–1811), *Reliques of Ancient English Poetry* (1765). Percy points out that this dragon was an overweight attorney who cheated some children of their estate and was made to disgorge by a local gentleman named More, who went against him, "armed with the spikes of the law," after which the dragon-attorney died of vexation.

4. Thoreau almost certainly refers here to an excursion Ralph Waldo Emerson took as a member of the "Adirondack Club"—an offshoot of the Saturday Club—to the Adirondack wilderness in August 1858. James Russell Lowell, Louis Agassiz, and Boston lawyer Horatio Woodman (1821–1870) were three members of the party. Emerson's poem "The Adirondacks" commemorates the trip, as does a painting by William James Stillman (1828–1901), now in the Concord Free Public Library, *The Philosophers' Camp in the Adirondacks* (1858).

5. "Attic salt" or "Attic wit" is a poignant, delicate wit peculiar to the Athenians of classical times in Greece.

6. The depot of the Fitchburg Railroad was located on the site now occupied by North Station, northwest of the junction of Causeway and Canal Streets in downtown Boston. The Gentlemen's Room presumably was a waiting room reserved for nonsmoking men.

7. In 1849 Emerson helped to organize the short-lived Town and Country Club, which met in Boston and was formed primarily "to afford a local habitation and dignified occupation" to the perpetually penniless idealist Amos Bronson Alcott. Thoreau is playing on the name "Town and Country" to refer to the more informal "club" of gentlemen like himself whose faces are set

westward, awaiting the next train out of town and into the countryside.

8. Thoreau first delivered "an extract from 'Autumnal Tints'" in Blake's parlors on Tuesday evening, February 22, 1859.

9. Born to a wealthy family, Henry James Sr. (1811–1882) was deeply committed to the mystical philosophy of Emanuel Swedenborg (1688–1772). James was the father of psychologist and philosopher William James (1842–1910) and writer and philosopher Henry James Jr. (1843–1916). As Abby Wolf has written, James believed that "egotism was the single most damaging force in the human personality, thwarting all attempts at connection and commonality. Emphasis on the self, to the exclusion or detriment of others, also made God remote from one's life. Without spiritual guidance, man retreats into himself . . . and so loses hold on his place in the outside world and his responsibility to it." James's communitarianism is the antithesis of Thoreau's individualism. An "Alcottian conversation" was an idealistic discussion after the fashion established by Amos Bronson Alcott wherein each participant advances the discussion with his or her own insights but is careful not to dominate or unduly complicate the discussion. Emerson described the dynamic in his journal entry of May 28, 1840: "[E]ach new speaker strikes a new light, emancipates us from the oppression of the last speaker to oppress us with the greatness & exclusiveness of his own thought, then yields us to another redeemer. . . ."

10. I have not been able to locate the event Thoreau refers to, although he may well be referring to a hypothetical instance of a criminal's "victim defense."

11. Very likely a generic last name. In the first chapter of *Walden*, Thoreau refers to "Dobson & Sons, stonecutters," but scholars have found no such company name in the directories of stonecutters. Likewise, scholars have found no inmate named Dobson in the local prison records of the time.

12. Doubtless Thoreau suggests here that the hypothetical Dobson

has "several times" told everyone within the sound of his voice to "go to hell."

13. Spanish for "golden man," El Dorado is a mythical country sought by early explorers of South America. The name is used figuratively to mean a place of fabulous wealth or a utopian dream.

14. A large glacial cirque on the east side of the southern slope of Mount Washington, named for Amherst College botany professor and world-renowned lichenologist Edward Tuckerman (1817–1886). Thoreau had read two of Tuckerman's treatises on lichens and had sprained his ankle during a bad fall while descending a brook in the ravine on July 9, 1858.

15. Genesis 13:12, "Abram dwelled in the land of Canaan, and Lot dwelled in the cities of the plain, and pitched his tent toward Sodom."

16. St. Augustine, Bishop of Hippo (A.D. 354–430), wrote a book titled *De Civitate Dei*, or *The City of God* (A.D. 426), which summarized his Christian philosophy of history.

17. French for Canada lynx (*Lynx canadensis*). Thoreau's use of the French reflects his wide reading in the literature of early French explorations of North America, a literature in which *loup-cerviers* are often mentioned.

18. The Saco River is about one hundred miles long, rises in the White Mountains, and flows southeast through Maine to the Atlantic Ocean. The Amazon River runs three thousand miles from the Andes Mountains to the Atlantic and is longer than any river but the Nile, which empties into the Mediterranean Sea in northeast Africa.

Letter Forty-four

1. As mentioned in note 7 to Letter 14, Apollo was banished from heaven and spent nine years tending the flocks of King Admetus.

2. As mentioned in note 8 to Letter 20 ("*Eastern War*"), the

Crimean War ended with the Treaty of Paris in March 1856. The principal battles of the Italian War of 1859 between the Austrians and the allied armies of France and Sardinia were Palestro (May 31), Magneta (June 4), and Solferino (June 24).

3. Whether or not to maintain a standing or full-time professional army—as opposed to relying on militias—for national defense was a critical question during the early days of the Republic, and many citizens continued to argue against such an army in Thoreau's day. He states his position on the matter in the opening paragraph of "Civil Disobedience," his most famous essay: "The objections which have been brought against a standing army, and they are many and weighty, and deserve to prevail, may also at last be brought against a standing government. The standing army is only an arm of the standing government."

4. Thoreau likely read about the legend of the Dead Sea apples in the annotation to book 10, line 562, in his edition of John Milton's great English epic, *Paradise Lost*, which annotation traces the story to the account given by the Jewish Roman historian Josephus (A.D. 37–100), who claimed that remnants of the trees of Sodom (north of the Dead Sea) "are still to be seen, as well as the ashes growing in their fruits, which fruits have a color as if they were fit to be eaten; but if you pluck them with your hands, they dissolve into smoke and ashes."

5. General Winfield Scott (1786–1866) in 1835 published *Infantry-Tactics; or, Rules for the Exercise and Manoeuvres of the United States' Infantry* in three volumes.

6. The elite bodyguard of Roman emperors.

7. In the 1830s warriors from the Zouaoua, a fiercely independent Kabyli tribe living in the hills of Algeria and Morocco, enlisted in the colonial French army, where they formed two battalions and were styled Zouaves. They were known for their valor in battle and colorful uniforms: short collarless jacket, sleeveless vest (*gilet*), voluminous trousers (*serouel*), twelve-foot woolen sash (*ceinture*), white canvas leggings (*guêtres*), leather greaves (*jambières*), and tasseled fez (*chéchia*) and turban (*chèche*). Zouave regi-

ments performed heroically during the Crimean War at the Battles of Alma, Inkermann, and Balaklava, and during the Siege of Sevastopol. Newspapers in England and America reported all of these battles in considerable detail, and Zouave accoutrements became fashionable in military circles. A few years later, for instance, gaily colored Zouave regiments of American soldiers marched off to fight in the American Civil War. "Pish!" is an exclamation of contempt, impatience, or disgust.

8. A poetical reference to the ocean shore. Thoreau probably intends an allusion to Matthew 7.7, "Ask, and it shall be given you; seek, and ye shall find; knock, and it shall be opened unto you." In his posthumously published book *Cape Cod*, he writes of looking into a shelter for shipwrecked passengers on the ocean's shore "with the eye of faith, knowing that, though to him that knocketh it may not always be opened, yet to him that looketh long enough ... the inside shall be visible. ..."

9. Near the end of *Cape Cod*, Thoreau writes, "In October, when the weather is not intolerably cold, and the landscape wears its autumnal tints, such as, methinks, only a Cape Cod landscape ever wears, especially if you have a storm during your stay,— that I am convinced is the best time to visit this shore."

10. Thoreau refers to the winds several times in the "Provincetown" chapter of *Cape Cod*, most humorously in connection to his nose: "What with wind and sun my most prominent feature fairly cast its slough."

11. The owners of land along the Concord River sued the proprietors of the Richardson mills in nearby Billerica for flooding their upriver hayfields by illegally raising the mills' dam over three feet. In June 1859 the landowners hired Thoreau to conduct a study of the river, its dams and bridge abutments, and he worked on the project assiduously throughout that month, submitting his survey on or about July 8, although he apparently continued studying the river for his own purposes throughout the remainder of the summer.

12. The Reverend Theodore Parker (1810–1860) was minister of

the Twenty-eighth Congregational Society, which met in Boston's Music Hall, but he had resigned the position for reasons of health in April 1859, after which time the society invited others to preach and lecture in Parker's stead. Thoreau delivered a lecture version of his posthumously published essay "Life without Principle" before the society at Music Hall on Sunday, September 5.

13. During a climb of Mount Wachusett in July 1859, Emerson had sprained his ankle badly enough to force him to cancel a planned vacation in Maine. The injury continued to bother him until January 1860.

Letter Forty-six

1. The general significance to Thoreau of the ideas of east ("E.") and west ("W.") is spelled out at some length in his essay "Walking" and may be summarized by the following extracts: "Eastward I go only by force; but westward I go free. Thither no business leads me. It is hard for me to believe that I shall find fair landscapes, or sufficient Wildness and Freedom behind the eastern horizon. . . .The West of which I speak is but another name for the Wild; and what I have been preparing to say is, that in Wildness is the preservation of the world."

2. In the Old Testament, a place near Jerusalem in the valley of Hinnom associated with the worship of the Canaanite god of fire, Moloch, to whom children were offered as burnt sacrifices. Now Tophet is synonymous with hell.

3. An interesting precursor to this idea is in Milton's *Paradise Lost*, book I, lines 254–55, where Satan soliloquizes, "The mind is its own place, and in itself / Can make a Heav'n of Hell, a Hell of Heav'n."

4. Thoreau actually used square brackets here, not parentheses.

5. As mentioned in note 3 to Letter 20, Atlas was a Titan and an ally of Kronos in the war against Zeus, who punished him for his

rebellion by condemning him to bear the heavens upon his shoulders.

6. Possibly an allusion to "Natura Naturans" by British poet Arthur Hugh Clough (1819–1861), line 61: "In Libyan dell the light gazelle. . . ."

7. Many old maps used this phrase to indicate unknown territory.

8. John Charles Frémont (1813–1890) and Elisha Kent Kane (1820–1857) were two of the most famous American explorers of Thoreau's time. Frémont explored the Great Basin in 1845, and Kane explored the Arctic regions on two expeditions sent out in 1850 and 1853–55 to find the British explorer Sir John Franklin (1786–1847) and his lost expedition.

9. The Great Basin, which was the last expanse in the continental United States to be explored during the nineteenth century, is the desert area bounded by the Sierra Nevada (west), the Columbia Plateau (north), the Rocky Mountains (east), and the Mojave and Sonoran Deserts (south). Polaris, or the North Star, is a fixed point by which explorers and navigators are able to determine their direction of movement.

10. Genesis 49:17, "Dan shall be a serpent by the way, an adder in the path, that biteth the horse heels, so that his rider shall fall backward."

11. A common expression preachers use at the completion of their sermons.

Letter Forty-eight

1. During Thoreau and Blake's June 1858 visit to Monadnock, the spruce house Thoreau built was just eighteen inches off the ground. One of these two new, more commodious spruce houses was built at the same location (see note 3 below); the other was built half a mile to the east-northeast.

2. That is, "you & Brown."

3. Several of the authors Thoreau read on early Native American

history use the phrase "chunk yard" to describe the public square around which lodges were built, and which were used for games and other tribal activities. In his journal Thoreau described the area where he and Blake built their camp in June 1858 as a "sunken yard in a rocky plateau on the southeast side of the mountain, perhaps half a mile from the summit, by the path, a rod and a half wide by as many more in length, with a mossy and bushy floor about five or six feet beneath the general level, where a dozen black spruce trees grew, though the surrounding rock was generally bare."

4. That is, "Channing declared." The "C" referred to elsewhere in this letter is also Channing.

5. Scottish poet Robert Burns (1759–1796) used this expression in his 1792 poem "The Rights of Women": "Now, thank our stars! those Gothic times are fled. . . ."

6. Thoreau mentions in his journal that many climbers of Monadnock carried chisels with them to engrave their names on the rocks at and around the summit. Many of these engravings are still discernible. Thoreau also mentions in his journal that residents of the area were drawn to ascend the mountain by the plentiful blueberries that grew on the slopes.

7. In Roman mythology, a "genius" is a tutelary deity or guardian spirit of place.

8. In the parable of the prodigal son, Luke 15:11–32, Jesus tells of a young man from a well-to-do family who had traveled "into a far country, and there wasted his substance with riotous living." On his return home, he confessed to his father that he was no longer worthy to be his son, but the father told his servants, "Bring forth the best robe, and put it on him; and put a ring on his hand, and shoes on his feet; and bring hither the fatted calf, and kill it; and let us eat and be merry: For this my son was dead, and is alive again; he was lost, and is found."

9. A "sound season" is synonymous with a "good time."

10. When Thoreau and his brother John first visited the White Mountains in 1839, they stayed at the Notch House, built in

1828 at Crawford Notch by Abel and Ethan Crawford and operated until 1854. This was a small inn, visitors to the area at this early date being too few to support a larger one. In 1837 Horace Fabyan opened Mount Washington House, which operated until 1951. The massive and lavishly appointed Crawford House, which opened at Crawford Notch in 1850 (rebuilt in 1859, operated until 1976), inaugurated a flurry of construction in the region, as did the decision that same year (1850) by the Atlantic & St. Lawrence Railroad to improve roads from its depot in Gorham, New Hampshire, southward to Pinkham Notch. In 1852 both the Glen House at Pinkham Notch and the Summit House on the mountain were built. The Tip-Top House, which is still standing, was built the following year; in 1854 a forty-foot "observatory" was built atop the summit rock; and in 1856 the Halfway House opened to serve the ever-increasing crowds of tourists.

11. I have not been able to determine this old farmer's identity.

12. The poem "Excelsior" by Henry Wadsworth Longfellow (1807–1882) was first published in 1841, became wildly popular, and was set to music by the well-known composer Michael William Balfe (1808–1870) in 1843. In the poem, a sad youth with a banner bearing the strange device "Excelsior" is encouraged by an old man, a maiden, and a peasant not to attempt a height in the Alps. When a hound discovered the hapless traveler lying "[l]ifeless, but beautiful" in the snow, "A voice fell, like a falling star, / Excelsior!"

13. The Whig Party came into being in 1834, led by three strikingly dissimilar senators with their own agendas: the "Great Triumvirate" of Henry Clay (1777–1852), Daniel Webster (1782–1852), and John C. Calhoun (1782–1850). By the presidential campaign of 1840 the party had become savvy enough to nominate a war hero candidate with no political baggage—and, alas, no experience. William Henry Harrison (1773–1841) campaigned on a platform without planks but with plenty of hype, slander, misrepresentation, and evasion.

Although Harrison had received a college education and grew up on a plantation worked by some two hundred slaves, his Democratic opponents dubbed him a "log cabin" candidate who was happiest on his backwoods farm sipping hard cider. Harrison's supporters enthusiastically seized on this image and promoted it in a number of colorful ways, distributing barrels of hard cider, for instance, and mounting several log cabins on floats for parades. The incident Thoreau recalls from the Harrison–Tyler "Log Cabin and Hard Cider" campaign of 1840 was doubtless one of many hundreds of such stunts in what has come to be regarded as the most raucus presidential campaign in American history.

14. Emerson climbed Monadnock on the morning of May 3, 1845, while his young friend Henry Thoreau was back in Concord building a small house and preparing a bean field near Walden Pond. Emerson began writing his poem "Monadnoc" that morning. In its final published form the narrator expresses surprise that southwestern New Hampshire, the region around the mountain, is the nursery not of "God's viceregency" or deputy but of a "squalid peasant." Later, however, the narrator considers that the regular folk of the area around the mountain are at work preparing "the bleak and howling place / For gardens of a finer race," tasks requiring what alone the mountain yields: "savage health and sinews tough." Thoreau suspects, then, that the "squalid peasant" of the poem was likely inspired by some of the folks Emerson met on the mountaintop rather than those he remembered in the valleys around the mountain.

15. An echo of Percy Bysshe Shelley's *Prometheus Unbound: A Lyrical Drama in Four Acts*, act 1, lines 41–43: "[F]rom their loud abysses howling throng / The genii of the storm . . . / . . . afflict me with keen hail. . . ."

16. Joseph Fassett (1795–1858) was born almost six miles south of Mount Monadnock, at Fitzwilliam, New Hampshire, where in 1820 he married Tabitha Wright, who bore him six sons and three daughters. The sons in November 1860 ranged in age from

thirty-nine (Joseph W. Fassett) to twenty-seven (Danvers C. Fassett). Interestingly, the father, Joseph, died from heart disease on September 17, 1858, just three months after Thoreau and Blake had visited the mountain. Joseph W., his oldest son, continued to live on the homestead at the southwestern base of the mountain after his father's death, continuing his father's project of erecting a "mountain house" on the southwestern slope above the family's homestead.

17. I have not been able to locate this story.

18. Fassett's moving of the "new castle" (mountain house) some thirty rods (about five hundred feet) downslope, where he "is still hammering," indicates that Thoreau is speaking—or at least thinks he is speaking—of a Fassett who was still alive at the time (November 1860). Thoreau may not have known that Joseph Fassett had died in 1858, so the infirmities he had heard of and might have assumed were the elder Fassett's may actually have been those of Fassett's oldest son, Joseph W., or perhaps one of Fassett's five younger sons. Whichever of the Fassetts he means, Thoreau's mention of Tap as Fassett's partner suggests that alcoholism was at the root of the man's infirmities.

19. In classical mythology, the three-headed watchdog guarding the gates of Hades, allowing the dead to enter, keeping the living out, and ensuring that no one left.

20. As part of its efforts to increase tourism to Mount Washington, the Atlantic & St. Lawrence Railroad built the Glen Bridle Path from Pinkham Notch to the summit, and at the bottom of the path in 1852 it built the Glen House. Contemporary photographs show a four-story peaked-roof wood-frame hotel, apparently painted white, situated atop a low ridge with the mountain rising behind and a porch running the entire breadth of the façade, which appears to be about three hundred feet.

21. The heaven of classical mythology, the place where the souls of the good went after death, a peaceful and beautiful region—and therefore by extension a place of supreme happiness.

22. Eighteen-year-old Albert Edward, Prince of Wales (1841–1910),

who became King Edward VII in 1901, was the first member of the British royal family to tour the United States. On September 21, 1860, after touring the Canadian provinces for seven weeks, the prince entered the United States at Detroit and then visited Chicago, St. Louis, Cincinnati, Baltimore, Washington, Richmond, Philadelphia, New York, Albany, and Boston before sailing from Portland, Maine, on October 20. In each city he visited the Prince was a guest in the residence of a prominent politician—in Washington (October 3–7), for instance, staying at the White House as a guest of President Buchanan (1791–1868), a bachelor. He visited Boston on October 17 and remained to the twentieth, the Boston newspapers covering every detail of his stay. The governor of Massachusetts greeted him at the train station and first introduced him to Edward Everett (1794–1865), who was at the time the vice presidential candidate of the Constitutional Union Party, with John Bell (1797–1869) of Tennessee, the presidential candidate. Everett was also a Unitarian clergyman, a professor of Greek literature at Harvard University, a well-known orator, the editor of the *North American Review,* a former governor of the state, and a former Harvard University president.

23. A sleeveless apronlike garment worn over a dress; usually spelled "pinafore," so called because they were formerly pinned "afore," or on the front of a dress.

24. An open flat-bottom boat with squared ends, used in shallow waters and usually propelled by a long pole.

25. Boys in New England made a game of climbing young birch trees and swinging the trees to the ground, the game consisting of seeing how high one could climb before the tree began bending. Robert Frost's famous poem "Birches" uses this game as its central trope.

26. Hebrews 12:22–23 (Douay Rheims), "But you are come to mount Sion, and to the city of the living God, the heavenly Jerusalem, and to the company of many thousands of angels. And to the church of the firstborn, who are written in the heavens, and to God the judge of all, and to the spirits of the just made perfect. . . ."

27. Commonly said to be the combined length of the average adult's small and large intestines.

28. Hebrews 11:9–10, "By faith he sojourned in the land of promise, as in a strange country, dwelling in tabernacles with Isaac and Jacob, the heirs with him of the same promise: For he looked for a city which hath foundations, whose builder and maker is God."

Acknowledgments

I AM GRATEFUL to the University of Texas Press and the Thoreau Society for generously granting me permission to reprint texts from their publications.

As always, I am especially delighted to recognize the contributions of my colleagues in Thoreau studies. I am grateful to Robert Hudspeth, who is editing Thoreau's complete correspondence in three volumes for *The Writings of Henry D. Thoreau*, for sharing with me several of his annotations; to Edmund A. Schofield and Pierre Monette for their assistance with several of the notes; to W. Barksdale Maynard and Dave Bonney for their timely telephone calls and invaluable encouragement; and to James Dawson for providing me with crucial documentation on short notice. Schofield, Maynard, Bonney, and Dawson also responded to drafts with helpful comments and suggestions, as did Chris Dodge and Richard Higgins. I very much appreciate the assistance of these six gentlemen. I also acknowledge with deep appreciation the masterful scholarship of Kenneth Walter Cameron, Lewis Hyde, Joseph J. Moldenhauer, Elizabeth Hall Witherell, and the staff of *The Writings of Henry D. Thoreau*.

The good people at W. W. Norton and Company were a joy to work with once again. Special thanks to Alane Mason for enthusiastic support of this project, Alessandra Bastagli for invaluable assistance in bringing it to fruition, and Amy Robbins for incredibly keen eyes and copyediting skills.

Finally, and most importantly, I acknowledge those wonderful souls most important to me and to whom I dedicate my labors on this project: my mother, Ida Mae; my father and stepmother, Fred and Kay; my son, David; and most especially she without whom I tremble to think what might become of me—my soulmate, best friend, and wife, Debra.

A Note to the Reader

IF YOU ENJOYED this collection of letters, you might consider joining the Thoreau Society. Founded in 1941, the Thoreau Society is the world's oldest and largest organization devoted to the legacy of an American author. Headquartered in Concord, Massachusetts, Thoreau's hometown and the village he described as "the most estimable place in all the world," the society draws its members from an unusually wide range of interests and professions. Society members include educators, scholars, and academics; religious, social, and political reformers, environmentalists and land preservationists, professionals in art history, natural history and science, and geography and urban planning; and, of course, writers and lovers of nature. What joins these diverse members together is their common support of a mission that honors Henry David Thoreau by stimulating interest in and fostering education about his life, works, and philosophy, and his place in his world and ours; by coordinating research on his life and writings; by acting as a repository for Thoreauviana and material relevant to Henry David Thoreau; and by advocating for the preservation of "Thoreau Country."

Under a contractual agreement with the Massachusetts Department of Conservation and Recreation, the Thoreau Society has been designated the commonwealth's sole official

Friends group for the Walden Pond State Reservation, which annually welcomes between 650,000 and 700,000 visitors from all over the world. Each summer, on the weekend closest to Thoreau's birthday (July 12), the society hosts an internationally visible meeting in Concord, Massachusetts. For many years the society has had an active and successful publications program: society publications include the annual journal the *Concord Saunterer,* the quarterly *Thoreau Society Bulletin,* and several reprints of classic books about Thoreau. The society also operates the very popular Shop at Walden Pond.

For more information about the Thoreau Society, including information about becoming a member, contact or visit:

The Thoreau Society
55 Old Bedford Road
Concord, Massachusetts 01742 U.S.A.

Tel.: (978) 369-5310
www.thoreausociety.org

not be heard.

Dec. 7th

That Walt Whitman, of whom I wrote to you, is the most interesting fact to me at present. I have just read his 2d edition (which he gave me) and it has done me more good than any reading for a long time. Perhaps you remember best the poem of Walt Whitman an American & the Sun Down Poem. There are 2 or 3 pieces in the book which are disagreeable to say the least, simply sensual. He does not celebrate love at all — it is as if the beasts spoke. I think that men have not been ashamed of themselves without reason. No doubt, there have always been dens where such deeds were unblushingly recited, and it is no merit to compete with their inhabitants. But even on this side, he has spoken more truth than any American or modern that I know. I have found his poems exhilarating encouraging. As for its sensuality, — & it may turn out to be less sensual than it appears — I do not so much wish that those parts were not written, as that men & women were so pure that they could read